Computer Craft 2

Updated Edition

Sarala Devi Dhanapal

ollins

Computer Craft 2

Updated Edition

Sarala Devi Dhanapal

Published by Collins Learning
A division of HarperCollins*Publishers* India Private Limited

HarperCollins *Publishers*
A-75, Sector 57, Noida, Uttar Pradesh 201301, India
1 London Bridge Street, London SE1 9GF, United Kingdom
2 Bloor Street East, Toronto, Ontario M4W 1A8, Canada
Lvl 13, 201 Elizabeth Street (PO Box A565, NSW, 1235), Sydney NSW 2000, Australia
195 Broadway, New York, NY 10007, USA

Browse the complete Collins catalogue at **www.collins.in**

For any queries/feedback, please write to us at
SCHOOLSUPPORT@harpercollins.co.in or call us on **0120-4044800**

First published in 2017
Latest updated edition 2018
Latest Reprinted edition 2020

Reprint 10 9 8 7 6 5 4

ISBN: 978-93-5277-1-783

Artwork, image research and layout by **Quadrum Solutions**, **Recto Graphics**

Cover layout by **Rahul Dhiman**

Printed and bound by MicroPrints India, New Delhi

Acknowledgements

Cover: Adyna

Title Page: Adyna

Preface

Computer Craft (Updated Edition) is a series of eight books for Classes 1 to 8. The course is based on Windows 7 and MS Office 2010 with updates on Office 365. This is a pedagogically mapped course that equips the students with theoretical and practical aspects of the subject.

It follows **Fink's Taxonomy**. This taxonomy imparts knowledge in all the three domains: *Cognitive*, *Affective* and *Psychomotor*. The progression of the series ensures that significant learning happens after thorough implementation of all the principles of Fink's Taxonomy. Thus, the learning outcomes of all topics ensure that the students have:

1. Foundational knowledge of the learning objectives
2. Sense of application of the learning objectives in their daily lives
3. Integration capabilities to relate computer science with other subjects
4. Valued group learning environment by identifying the areas that need improvement
5. Developed new interests and curiosity to learn more about the subject
6. Become self-directed learners by learning how to think in the right direction

The structural design of the course facilitates comprehensive learning and understanding of the basic concepts and applications of Computer Science. The course is interspersed with illustrations, keyboard shortcuts and facts. The series covers MS Office 2010 and programming languages like BlueJ and Java.

Some Key Features

The key features of the series like **Lab Activities** and **Projects** are given with the aim of inducing curiosity and familiarizing the students with practical applications of the topics. Sections like

- **You Should Know**
- **Keyboard Shortcuts**
- **Summary**
- **Word Web**
- **Teacher's Notes**
- **Lab Activity**

cover the details of the concepts through each dimension.

To enable the students face the challenges and to provide them a competitive edge by developing their lateral thinking and analytical skills, following sections are given in each book:

- **Worksheets**
- **Assessments**
- **Projects**
- **Revision Questions**
- **National Cyber Olympiad by Science Olympiad Foundation – for Classes 3 to 8**

Collins DigiSuite is an interactive digital solution which provides an e-book with learning materials and interactive teaching tools that will help the teachers to prepare additional notes and practice questions for students.

I would like to thank all the teachers who have reviewed the series and have contributed to inspire the learners today. I sincerely welcome constructive feedback and suggestions to improve these books further in subsequent editions.

Author

Key Features

Word Web

Explains the difficult words

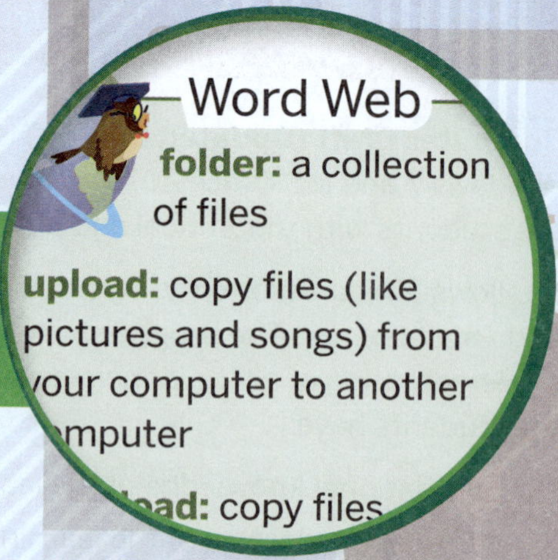

You Should Know

Gives interesting facts about the topic

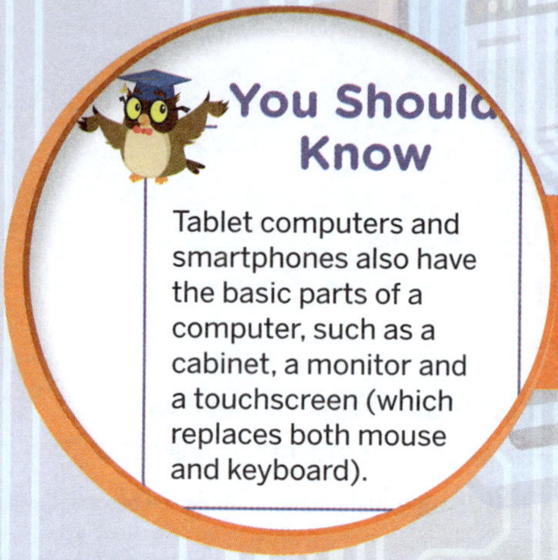

Keyboard Shortcuts

Highlight all the important keyboard shortcuts for the menu commands

Exercise

Reinforces the understanding of the topic

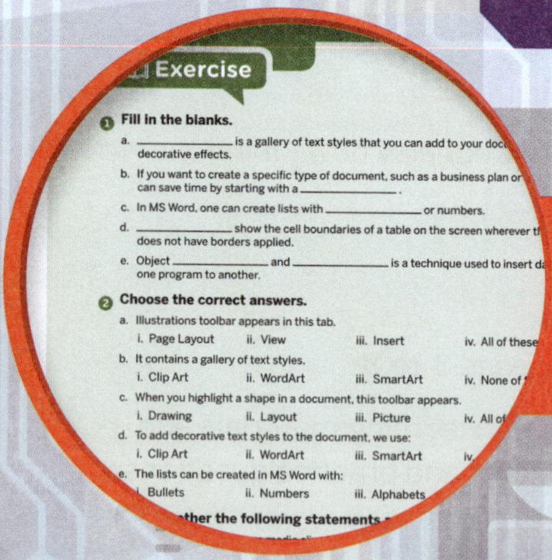

National Cyber Olympiad

Actual question paper by Science Olympiad Foundation

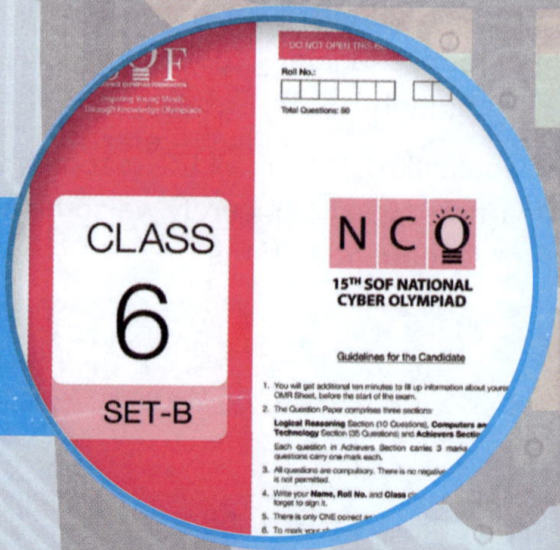

Worksheets

Reinforce the concepts by testing student's grasping power

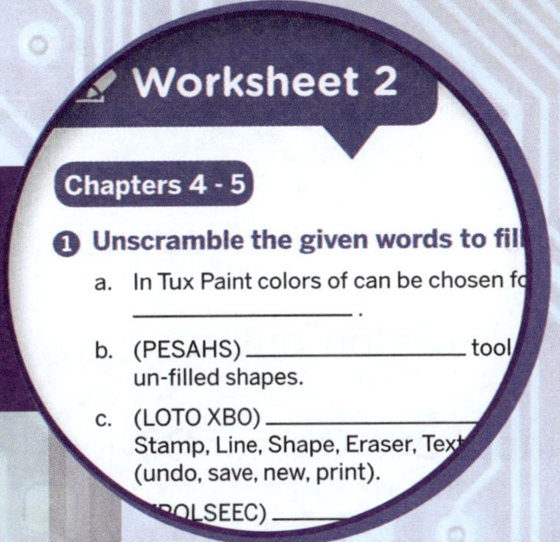

Worksheet 2

Chapters 4 - 5

1 Unscramble the given words to fill

a. In Tux Paint colors of can be chosen fo
_______________ .

b. (PESAHS) _______________ tool
un-filled shapes.

c. (LOTO XBO) _______________
Stamp, Line, Shape, Eraser, Text
(undo, save, new, print).

Assessments

Facilitate the students and teachers with additional questions

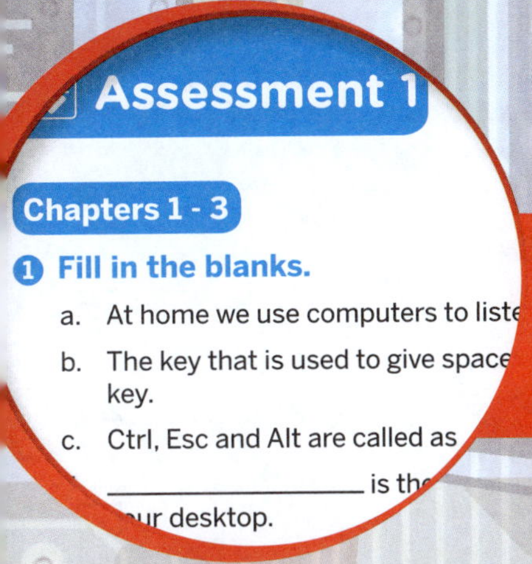

Assessment 1

Chapters 1 - 3

1 Fill in the blanks.

a. At home we use computers to liste

b. The key that is used to give space
key.

c. Ctrl, Esc and Alt are called as

_______________ is th
ur desktop.

Revision Questions

Aim at testing students' understanding of the concepts taught

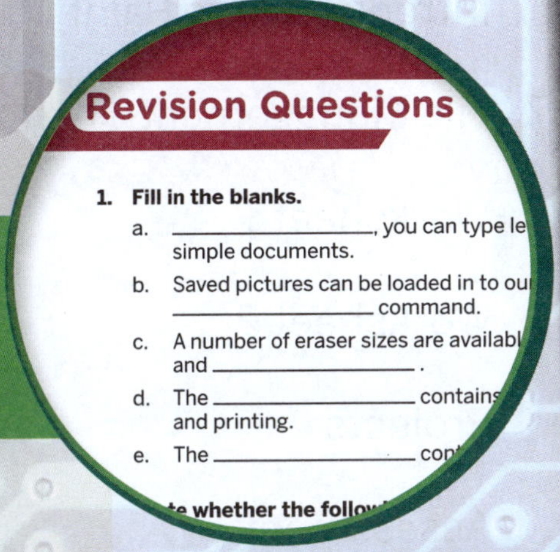

Revision Questions

1. Fill in the blanks.

a. _______________, you can type le
simple documents.

b. Saved pictures can be loaded in to ou
_______________ command.

c. A number of eraser sizes are availabl
and _______________ .

d. The _______________ contains
and printing.

e. The _______________ con

Projects

Integrate Computer Science with other subjects, wherever possible

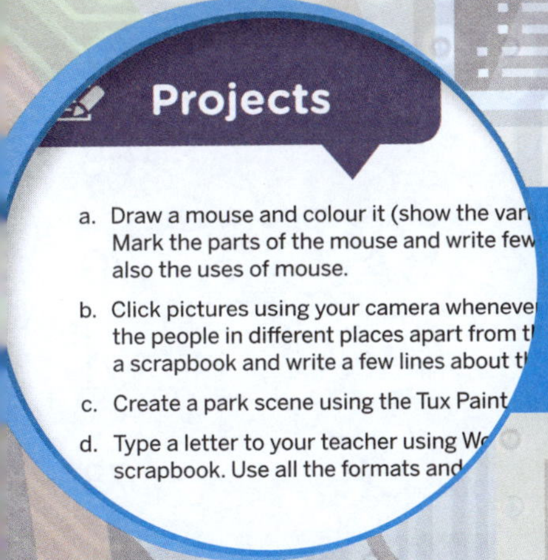

Projects

a. Draw a mouse and colour it (show the var
Mark the parts of the mouse and write few
also the uses of mouse.

b. Click pictures using your camera wheneve
the people in different places apart from t
a scrapbook and write a few lines about t

c. Create a park scene using the Tux Paint

d. Type a letter to your teacher using W
scrapbook. Use all the formats and

Collins DigiSuite is an innovative digital solution for teachers. It contains four modules delivering classroom content that can be used to effectively integrate the teaching and evaluation tools with the coursebooks.

The **E-book** includes animations, interactive exercises and worksheets. The E-book reader also includes interactive teaching tools like pen tool, text highlighter, page zoom, search and bookmark.

The **Test Generator** is a question bank with a variety of questions for effective evaluation. It is an easy-to-use assessment tool for the teachers to create test papers and worksheets.

The **Teacher's Resource** consists of lesson plans, answer keys and teaching techniques for the teachers.

This module has a PDF of the **Collins dictionary** appropriate for each level with all the words and definitions one needs.

Contents

1.	Computer—An Electronic Device	7
2.	Role of Computers	13
3.	Input and Output Devices	21
4.	Keyboard—Special Keys	28
5.	Mouse—an Input Device	35
6.	Introduction to Paint	41
7.	File Management—An Introduction	57
	Worksheet 1	63
	Worksheet 2	65
	Projects	67
	Assessment 1	68
	Assessment 2	70
	Revision Questions	71
	Computer Manners	73
	Additional Software	74
	Exploring IT Personalities	76

   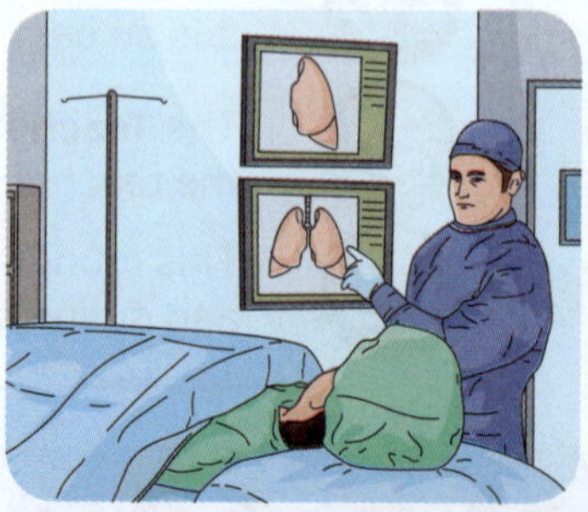

Computer—An Electronic Device

1

What I shall learn

- Computers are an electronic device
- Computers and humans have different ways of working
- Advantages and disadvantages of using computer

A computer is an electronic machine that processes information. It takes in data as the input, stores it until it's ready to work on it, and then processes it to give the results as the output.

Computers and Humans

A computer is an electronic machine which helps us to do many things. But, is this machine different from human beings in any way?

Yes, it is.

A computer can do many tasks at a time

A computer can do many difficult tasks at the same time. It is called 'multitasking'.

Humans cannot do multiple tasks at the same time.

For example, counting backwards, multiplying 2 numbers and addition of two numbers is possible to do at the same time by a computer but a human can do it one by one at different time.

Word Web

Electronic device: a device that controls the flow of current.

A computer is faster at doing any work.

Computer can do fast calculations than humans. It can do many calculations within a few seconds.

A computer does not make mistakes.

Computer gives correct answer while solving problems. Sometimes, humans make mistakes.

A computer can memorize many things without any effort.

Computer can memorize anything without any effort and remember for a long time. Humans needs more time and effort to memorize anything and may forget after sometime.

A computer neither gets tired nor gets bored in doing the same work again and again.

Humans get bored and tired when they have to do the same work repeatedly.

Computers are machines, they do exactly what the humans want it to do.

A computer cannot decide on its own.

Computers cannot decide on their own to do any task. Humans take their own decisions.

Computers have no emotions like humans. So, it will never feel happy or sad.

Thus, there are many differences between computers and humans.

You Should Know

Humans get energy from food like fruits, vegetables, milk etc. Computer gets energy through electricity.

Advantages of computer

- A computer is very fast. It solves sums very quickly.
- A computer always gives correct answers. It does not make mistakes.
- A computer has a huge memory. It can be used to store a lot of data.
- A computer makes our work easy and simple.
- A computer is very quick. It saves our time.
- A computer never gets tired.
- A computer is used to give electronic presentation.
- A computer is used by the teachers in schools for teaching the subjects using e-boards.
- A computer is used by the students to search information on any subject on the internet.

Disadvantages of computer

- A computer performs different tasks automatically without any humans help.
- Young generation is now spending more time on the websites like Facebook, Twitter etc. or texting their friends through smartphones which is bad for both studies and their health.
- A computer is used to do wrong activities like stealing the credit card or debit card numbers of the people and misuse them.
- An improper usage of computer and for a long time will results in injuries or disorders of hands, wrists, elbows, eyes, necks and back.

Word Web

Texting: messaging

Disposed: set out

You Should Know

Computer waste which is also called as E-waste (Environmental waste) are polluting the environment. The wasted parts of computer can release dangerous poisonous materials.

'Green computer' is a method to reduce the electricity consumed and environmental waste generated when using a computer. The used computers must be donated or disposed off properly.

Summary

1. A computer is an electronic machine that takes in data as input, processes it and gives out output.
2. Computers are faster than humans.
3. Computers are always correct.
4. Computers do not have any emotions.
5. Computers cannot take decisions.
6. There are many advantages and disadvantages of using a computer.

Teacher's Notes

- Discuss how a computer is an electronic device which processes information based on given instructions.
- Explain the working of computer and compare it with the way humans work.
- Discuss the advantages and disadvantages of a computer.

Exercise

1 Fill in the blanks.

a. A computer is an electronic machine that processes ______________.

b. A computer does not make ______________.

c. A computer cannot take ______________ on its own.

d. A computer performs different ______________ without any humans help.

e. Computer waste is also called as ______________.

2 Unscramble the words.

a. E C L T O I C E R N

b. U P N I T

c. R O P C S E S

d. P T O U T U

e. I S E D C N O I

3 State whether the following statements are true (T) or false (F).

a. A computer is very quick.

b. Texting friends through smartphones is good for both studies and their health.

c. A computer does not get bored.

d. A computer does not have memory.

e. A computer is sometimes correct but not always.

4 Answer the following questions

a. Why is computer called an electronic machine?

b. Write any 3 advantages and disadvantages of a computer.

____

____

____

c. What is e-waste?

____

____

____

d. Define the term 'Green Computer'.

____

____

____

Role of Computers

2

What I shall learn

- Understand the uses of computers in schools, homes, airports, railway stations, hospitals, offices, banks and shops

You've already studied that, computers have made our lives better and easier. They are used in different fields of work.

Computers are used at many places such schools, airports, railways stations, hospitals, banks, hotels and offices. Computers are used to do different tasks at different places. Engineers, architects, jewellers and film-makers all use computers to design things.

Word Web

online: connected to the Internet

Teachers, writers and most office workers use computers for doing research, typing documents and emailing.

Let us study some of the uses of a computer.

At Home

We use computers for different purposes at home. Some of the uses are given below:

1. Computers are used to type text.
2. Computers are used to do online shopping.
3. Computers are used to talk to friends and family.
4. Computers are used to watch movies.
5. Computers are used to play and record music.
6. Computers are used to play games.

Fig. 2.1 To type text

Fig. 2.2 To do online shopping

You Should Know

Computers are also used by soldiers during wartime.

Fig. 2.3 To talk to friends and family

Fig. 2.4 To watch videos

Fig. 2.5 To play and record music

Fig. 2.6 To play games

You Should Know

Computers also help in managing office work from home. One can talk to clients in faraway locations using computers. Further, companies can even interact with and manage their employees working from home.

In Offices, Banks and Shops

Computers are used in offices, banks and shops to perform the following functions:

1. Computers are used to type letters, reports and bills.
2. Computers are used to store customer, employee and bank details in a bank.
3. Computers are used to withdraw money from an Automated Teller Machine (ATM).

Fig. 2.7 To type letters, reports and bills

Fig. 2.8 To store customer, employee and bank details in a bank

Fig. 2.9 To withdraw money from an Automated Teller Machine (ATM)

At Railway Stations and in Airports

Computers are used in railway stations and airports:

1. To book tickets
2. To provide timings of trains and aeroplanes, and other information like passenger details

Fig. 2.10 To book air tickets

Fig. 2.11 To book rail tickets

In Schools

Computers are used in schools to teach using interactive videos, worksheets and programs. The students also use computers to learn different subjects.

Computers also help in organizing questions and thus, in preparing test papers.

Computers are also used in school libraries to keep record of the books. The attractive notices, circulars and time-tables that you see in the school are prepared and printed using computers.

Computers keep and update fee records of the students. They are also used to maintain student records.

Fig. 2.12 To teach

Fig. 2.13 To prepare test papers

Word Web

interactive: allowing interaction between a computer and its user

symptoms: signs

prescribed: given by a doctor

automate: computerize

procedures: activities

In Hospitals

Computers are used in hospitals to store the details of patients, their diseases, symptoms and the medicines that are prescribed to them.

Computers are also used to automate the day-to-day procedures and operations in a hospital.

They are used to prepare medical reports and bills of the patients. Many devices that are used by disabled people use computers or computing technology. For example, Braille keyboards are used by the blind.

Word Web

Braille keyboard: a special keyboard that helps the blind to type

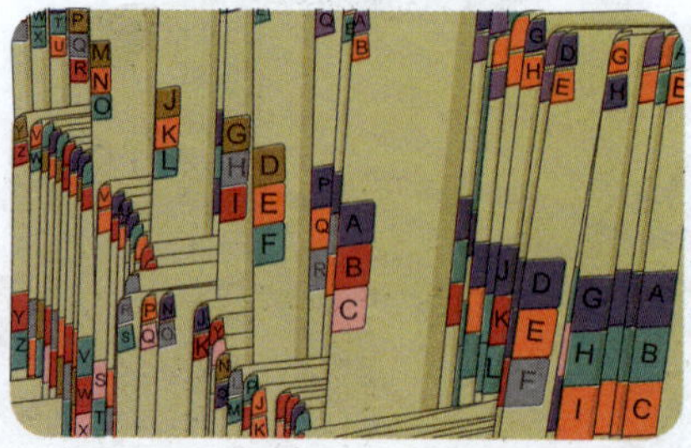

Fig. 2.14 Folders arranged in alphabetical order

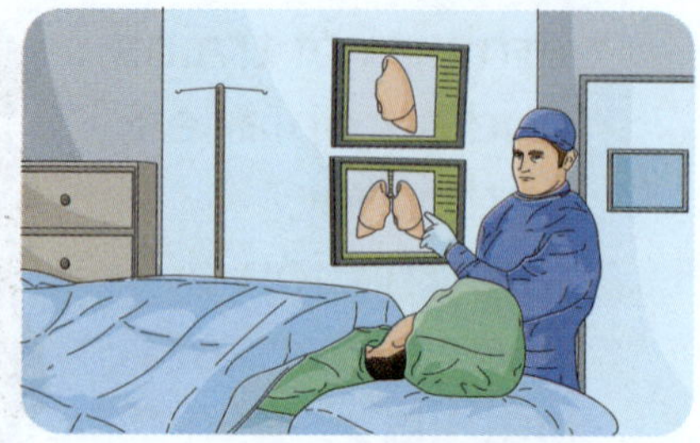

Fig. 2.15 To automate procedures and operations

For Making Movies

Computers also help us to make movies.

You must have seen movies like *Kung Fu Panda* and *Shrek*. These movies are called **animated movies** that were created using the computers. Animated movies and cartoon films show drawings of people and animals which seem to move.

Fig. 2.16 Computer used for making animated movies

Apart from the uses that you've studied so far, computers are also used in the designing field. The clothes that you wear, are designed by the fashion designers using the computers.

The buildings, bridges and the flyovers that you see are designed using the computers by the architects.

The engineers, artists and publishers – all use computers to design cars, airplanes, machines, artwork, books, magazines and newspapers.

Fig. 2.17 Computer used to design clothes

Fig. 2.18 Computer used by architects

Fig. 2.19 Computer used by publisher

Studying Space

Computers help us take photographs of the stars and the planets.

Computers provide data about other planets through satellites.

Fig. 2.20: Computers used to study space

Computers help us launch and control satellites and rockets used in space research.

Fig. 2.21: Computers used to launch and control satellites

Computers also help in weather forecasting and monitoring the temperature.

Summary

1. Computers are used in different fields of work.
2. At home, we can play games, watch movies, draw pictures and talk to friends using computers.
3. We use computers in offices, shops and banks to type letters and bills, store details of customers and withdraw money.
4. ATMs (Automated Teller Machines) are computers which are used to withdraw and deposit money.
5. Computers are used in railway stations and airports for booking tickets and providing passenger details.
6. Computers are used in schools to teach and prepare test papers.
7. Computers are used in hospitals to store patients' details and automate operations.
8. Computers are used by the fashion designers to design clothes.
9. Computers are used by the publishers to design books, magazines and newspapers.
10. Computers are used for studying space, forecasting weather and launching and controlling satellites.

Teacher's Notes

- Discuss the things that a computer can do.
- Ask the students to list the places where they have seen computers in use.
- Discuss the various uses of a computer in a particular place.
- Inform that the computers are also used in weather forecasting, space research, etc.

Exercise

1 Fill in the blanks.

a. Computers have made our lives ______________ and ______________.

b. We can watch ______________ on a computer.

c. We can play ______________ on a computer.

d. Computers are used to book ______________ in railways stations.

e. Computers are used in ______________ to store patients' details.

2 Unscramble the given words.

a. P I A L H S O T ______________

b. H S O L O C ______________

c. T A I P O R R ______________

d. N K B A ______________

e. F O F C I E ______________

3 State whether the following statements are true (T) or false (F).

a. A computer can only be used in the schools. ☐

b. Doctors do not ever use a computer. ☐

c. Computers are used in designing field. ☐

d. We can make movies using the computers. ☐

e. A computer cannot be used in ATMs. ☐

4 Answer the following questions.

a. List some of the uses of computers in the following places.

i. At home ______________

ii. In offices ______________

iii. In airports ______________

iv. In schools ______________

b. How are computers used in hospitals?

____

____

c. What is the full-form of ATM?

____

____

d. Why do we use computers in the schools?

____

____

e. List the uses of the computers in designing field.

____

____

____

Input and Output Devices

3

What I shall learn

- Understand the workflow in a computer
- Learn about computer hardware and software
- Know about various parts of a computer

Introduction

A **computer** is an electronic device that

1. accepts and stores the input data,
2. processes the input data,
3. generates output in the required format.

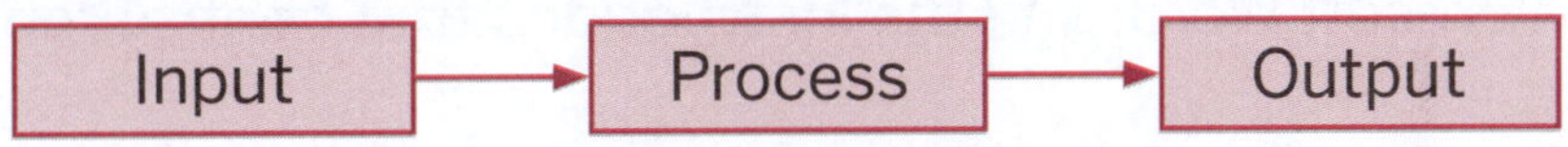

Fig. 3.1 Workflow in a computer

This cycle is often known as the IPO (Input – Process – Output) cycle. Various parts of the computer are involved in the IPO cycle.

The parts of a computer can be divided into two major categories: hardware and software.

Hardware

Hardware refers to the physical parts of a computer, that is the parts which we can see and touch.

Fig. 3.2 Hardware

The devices used to enter data into a computer are called input devices. Keyboard, mouse, scanner and digital camera are some of the common input devices.

The processed data can be presented to the users with the help of output devices. Monitor, printer, speakers and headphones are examples of output devices.

All the input and output devices form part of the hardware of the computer.

Software

Software is a collection of instructions that are given to a computer. These instructions tell the computer what to do.

Software is not a physical object, but it can be stored in a physical medium such as a CD-ROM. It is just a set of instructions to do a particular task. These instructions are written in a programming language.

Fig. 3.3 Logo of Linux OS

You Should Know

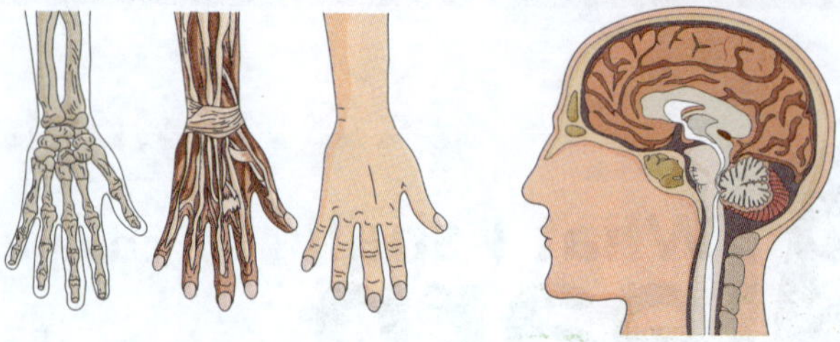

Computer hardware and software can also be understood by comparing these to the human body. Bones, muscles, skin, blood and other physical parts of the body are the hardware, whereas our thoughts and mental processes are the software as these are the set of instructions that tell our physical body what to do.

Operating systems such as Windows XP and Mac OS X, applications such as Microsoft Word, and the instructions that control robots are all examples of software.

Parts of a Computer

Let us discuss the various parts of a desktop computer in detail.

Mouse

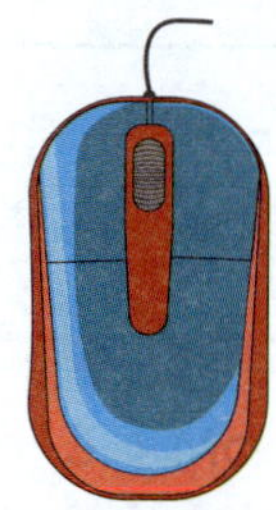

Fig. 3.4 Mouse

Mouse is the most commonly used pointing or cursor-control input device. It is a small, palm-sized box with a ball at its base. This ball senses the movement of the mouse and sends signals to the CPU for relevant mouse actions, when the mouse buttons are pressed.

Nowadays, optical mouse are more popular. They make use of light sensors to sense the movement of the mouse on the mouse pad and accordingly move the cursor on the screen.

A mouse has two buttons (the left and the right buttons) and a scroll wheel between them.

A mouse is used to move the cursor on the screen. The advantages of a mouse are:

1. It is easy to use.
2. It is not very expensive.
3. It moves the cursor faster than the arrow keys of the keyboard.

Keyboard

Keyboard is a popular input device that helps in entering data into the computer.

The layout of the keyboard is like that of a traditional typewriter, although the keyboard has some additional keys for performing extra functions.

Fig. 3.5 Keyboard

The most commonly used keyboards have 104 keys. Such keyboards are also known as QWERTY keyboards because the alphabet keys are arranged in QWERTY sequence.

Monitor

Monitor, also known as the Visual Display Unit (VDU), is the main output device of a computer.

It forms images from tiny dots called **pixels** that are arranged in rows and columns. The sharpness of an image depends upon the number of pixels.

Fig. 3.6 CRT and TFT Monitors

There are two types of monitors:

1. Cathode Ray Tube (CRT) monitors
2. Thin Film Transistor (TFT) monitors

Speakers and Headphones

Speakers and headphones receive audio input from the computer and produce audio output in the form of sound. They are the audio components of a computer.

Speakers are used to produce audio loud enough to be heard from a distance. Headphones are used when you want to listen to an audio without disturbing others.

Fig. 3.7 Speakers and headphones

Cabinet

The **cabinet** has all the main components of a computer. It is also called the **computer case** or **computer tower**. It is the box that holds the **Central Processing Unit** (CPU), which acts as the brain of the computer. The unit contains the motherboard, which is the main part of the cabinet.

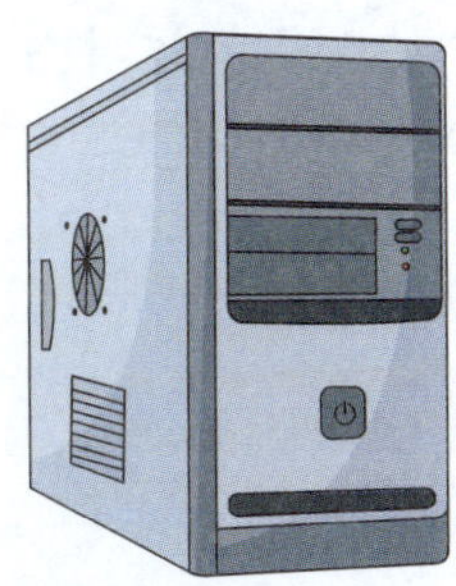

Fig. 3.8 Cabinet

Printer

Fig. 3.9 Printer

Printer is the most popular output device used to produce a document or a picture on a paper.

Any text that is difficult to read on the monitor screen can be printed to read with ease on a paper.

You Should Know

The printed copy of some information is known as the hard copy, whereas the digital copy that you see on the computer monitor is known as the soft copy.

Compact Disc (CD) and Digital Versatile Disc (DVD)

Fig. 3.10 CD and DVD

A **compact disc** (CD) is a small, portable and round-shaped disc used to record, store and playback audio, video, text and other information in digital form.

CDs are popular for music recording and playback. A newer technology, the digital versatile disc (DVD), has more storage space and is popularly used for playing back movies.

Pen Drive

Fig. 3.11 Pen drive

Pen drive is a portable storage device. It is used to store information from a computer and use it on another computer. It is also known as flash drive or thumb drive.

Scanner

Fig. 3.12 Scanner

Scanner is an input device that works like a photocopy machine. It is used when some information is available on paper and it needs to be transferred on to the computer.

A scanner captures images from the source which are converted into the digital form.

In other words, hard copy gets converted into soft copy. These scanned images can then be stored on the disc. These can also be edited before they are printed again.

Summary

1. A computer is an electronic device that accepts data, stores it, processes it and generates output.
2. The parts of a computer are divided into two major categories: hardware and software.
3. Hardware refers to the physical parts of a computer, whereas software refers to the instructions given to a computer to do some work.
4. There are various parts of a desktop computer like mouse, keyboard, monitor, speakers and headphones, cabinet, CD and DVD, pen drive, and scanner.
5. Data is the information fed into computer using input devices.
6. The output devices show the result of the data fed to the users.

Lab Activity

Make a list of the input and output devices found in your school computer lab. Try to collect their pictures and paste them in your scrapbook.

Teacher's Notes

- Introduce the computer with its definition.
- Describe the two major divisions of computer parts: hardware and software.
- Show the pictures of the various parts of a computer.
- Describe the functions of each part.
- Discuss how to use the various parts.
- Let students observe the various parts of a computer like mouse, keyboard, printer, etc. in the computer lab.
- Let students know the difference between input and output devices.

Exercise

1 Fill in the blanks.

a. A computer is an ________________ device.

b. The two major categories of computer parts are ________________ and ________________.

c. Mouse is the most commonly used ________________ device.

d. The layout of the keyboard is like that of a traditional ________________.

e. Printer is a device used to produce ________________ output.

2 Name the following.

a. A newer technology that stores much more information and is used for playing back movies ________________

b. The parts of a computer that you can see and touch ________________

c. Tiny dots that form images on a monitor ________________

d. The device that works like a photocopy machine ________________

e. A small, palm-sized box with a ball at its base ________________

3 State whether the following statements are true (T) or false (F).

a. Hardware is a collection of instructions. ☐

b. Mouse is the most commonly used cursor-control device. ☐

c. The cabinet holds the CPU, which acts as the brain of the computer. ☐

d. A mouse has three buttons. ☐

e. A scanner captures images from the source, which are then converted into digital form. ☐

4 Answer the following questions.

a. Define the following terms.

i. Hardware ii. Software iii. Input devices iv. Output devices

____

____

____

b. Name any five parts of a desktop computer.

c. Expand the following.

i. CPU ii. CD iii. DVD

d. State the advantages of a mouse.

e. Explain briefly what is a pen drive.

Keyboard—Special Keys

4

What I shall learn

- Different groups of keys on a keyboard
- Functions of typing keys, special keys and functions keys
- How to use the numeric keypad

Introduction

A keyboard is an input device used to communicate with a computer. It has numbers and letters. Without a keyboard, we cannot enter our name, address or phone number into the computer. A keyboard is required to type data into a computer.

A computer keyboard closely resembles a typewriter keyboard. Apart from the keys that the typewriter has, a computer keyboard has additional keys. These additional keys are used for special functions.

The keys on a keyboard can be divided into several groups based on functions (Fig. 4.1).

Word Web

input device: a device used to enter data into a computer

resembles: looks like

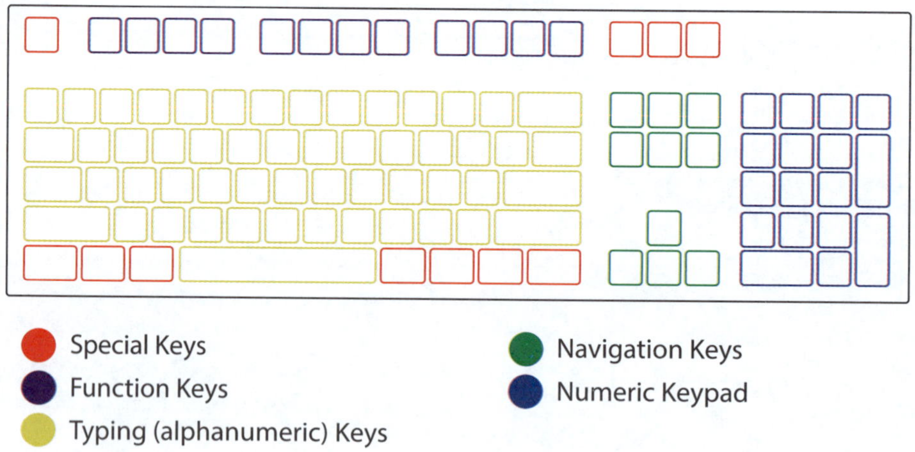

Fig. 4.1 Different groups of keys on a keyboard

Let us look at each type of key on a keyboard.

Typing Keys

There are various kinds of typing keys.

Number Keys and Symbol Keys

The **number keys** are used to type numbers: 0, 1, 2, 3, 4, 5, 6, 7, 8 and 9.

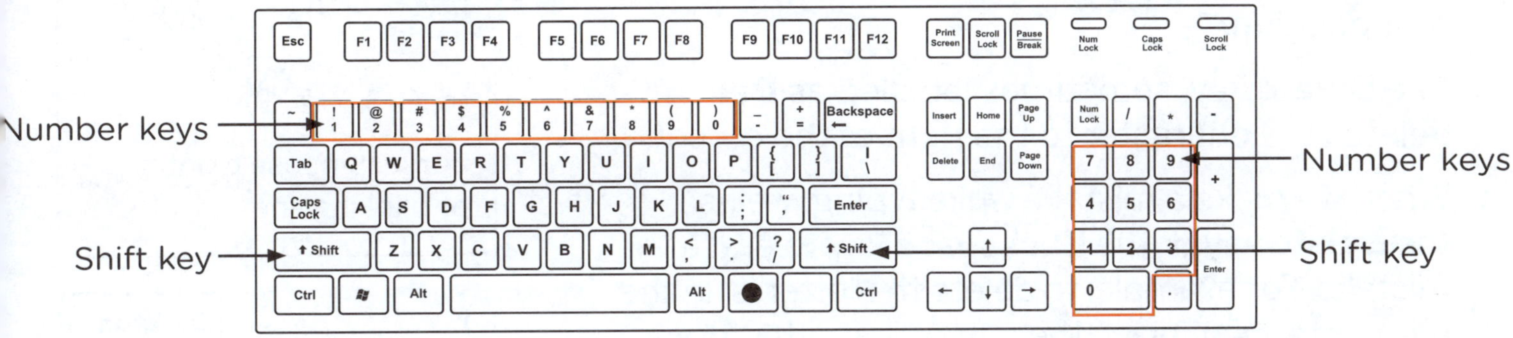

Fig. 4.2 Number keys

They are found in the row of keys above the first row of letters. Another set of number keys is present on the extreme right-corner of the keyboard as shown in Fig. 4.2.

Also written on the number keys are various symbols, such as $, & and *. To use these, hold down the **Shift** key while typing. So, if we press '7', we get '7', but if we press '7' while holding down the **Shift** key, we get '&'.

There are some more symbol keys found on the keyboard (Fig. 4.3).

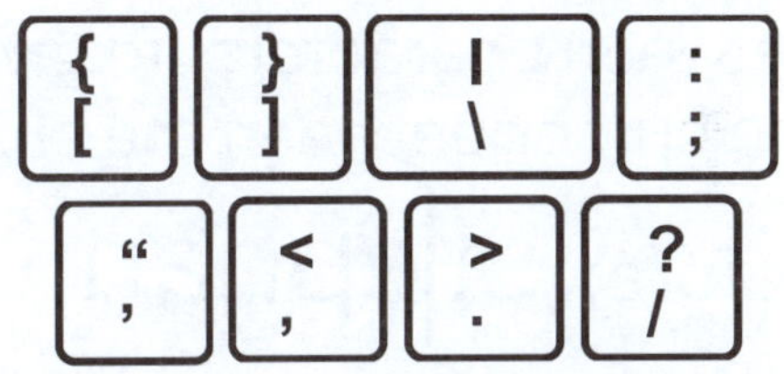

Fig. 4.3 Other symbol keys on the keyboard

You Should Know

1. To type the symbol given near the top edge of the key, press the required key with the Shift key.
2. By default, the Caps Lock key is switched off.

Word Web

lower case: small letters

upper case: capital letters

Alphabet Keys

The keys with letters from A to Z are called **alphabet keys**. These are used to type text. When we type using these keys, we get the letters in lower case. However, if we hold down the **Shift** key and type, we get the letters in upper case. We can also press the **Caps Lock** key once and then type to get the letters in upper case.

Fig. 4.4 Use the Shift key to type letters in upper case

Backspace Key and Delete Key

The **Backspace** key deletes the character to the left of the cursor and moves the cursor to that position.

The **Delete** key, sometimes labelled as **Del**, deletes the character to the right of the cursor.

When we make a mistake while typing, we use the **Delete** key or the **Backspace** key to erase the mistake. For example, to delete the letter 's' in the name 'stephen', place the cursor just after 's' and press the **Backspace** key once. Or, you can place the cursor just before 's' and press the **Delete** key once.

Word Web

character: a letter, a number or a symbol (d, G, 3, 7, @, $)

cursor: mouse pointer or blinking line

s|tephen [Backspace ←]

|stephen [Delete]

Spacebar Key

The longest key on the keyboard is the **Spacebar** key. It is used to give spaces between characters. To give a single blank space between two characters, place the cursor between the characters and press the **Spacebar** key once.

Before: st|ephan After: st |ephan

You Should Know

Some keyboards, especially those of laptops, have a different arrangement of keys. For example, there might be only one set of number keys instead of two. The Delete key might be in a different place on the keyboard, and there might be only one Enter key. But all keyboards necessarily have all these important keys.

Navigation Keys

Navigation keys are also known as **arrow keys**.
These keys are used to move the cursor on the screen and are also known as cursor control keys.

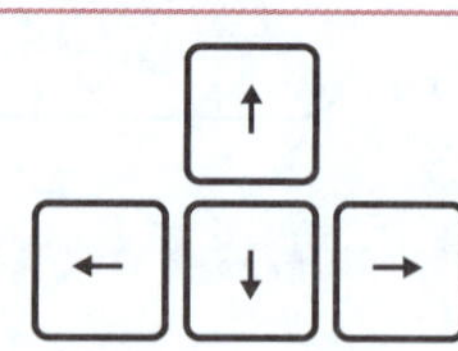

Fig. 4.5
Navigation Keys

Special Keys

Ctrl Key, Alt Key and Esc Key

You've already studied about various types of special keys in previous class. Let us now study about some of them in detail.

The **Control (Ctrl)** key and the **Alternate (Alt)** key are special keys that are used in combination with other keys. These keys are used to perform specific functions.

Fig. 4.6 Ctrl and Alt keys

For example, if we press **Ctrl**, **Alt** and **Delete** at the same time, a menu will open.

Fig. 4.7 Esc key

The **Escape (Esc)** key is used to exit (or escape) from programs and tasks.

Function Keys

Special keys labelled from **F1** to **F12** are the **Function** keys. These keys have different functions depending on which program is running.

Fig. 4.8 Function keys

Numeric Keypad

It is used to type numbers. To use the numeric keypad, press the **Num Lock** key.

An **indicator light** at the top of the keyboard or on the **Num Lock** key itself will show that it is on.

Fig. 4.9 Numeric keypad

You Should Know

Look at the keyboard below. This is the ideal placement of fingers for typing on a keyboard.

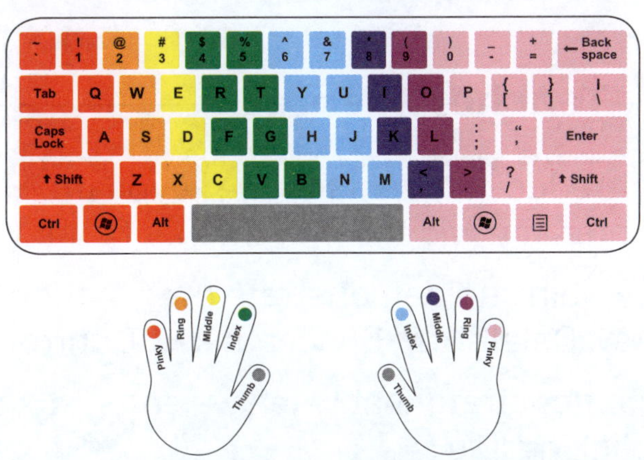

Hands-on Practice

Try typing the following sentence using a keyboard. Colour the keys in red that you pressed to type this sentence.

Last night, I won ₹ 98,76,54,321 in a jackpot!

Summary

1. A keyboard is an input device used to communicate with a computer.
2. There are different groups of keys on a keyboard: typing keys, control keys, function keys and numeric keypad.
3. Number keys (0-9), punctuation keys (like ! , . ?), alphabet keys (A-Z), Backspace key, Delete key and Spacebar key are the typing keys.
4. Control keys are Ctrl, Alt and Esc.
5. To use the numeric keypad, press the Num Lock key.

Teacher's Notes

- Introduce students to the keyboard. Help them recall the functions of the Enter key and the movement of cursor using the arrow keys learnt in Class 1.
- Explain and demonstrate the functions of different keys: Shift key, Backspace key, Delete key, Spacebar key, Control key, Alt key, Escape key and Num Lock key.
- Demonstrate that when we enter text the cursor changes into a flashing or blinking line.

Exercise

1 Fill in the blanks.

a. A computer keyboard closely resembles a ______________ keyboard.

b. A keyboard is required to enter ______________ in a computer.

c. We can type in upper case by holding down the ______________ key.

d. ______________ keys are used to type letters from A to Z.

e. The numeric keypad works only when the ______________ key is pressed.

2 Label the different groups of keys on the given keyboard.

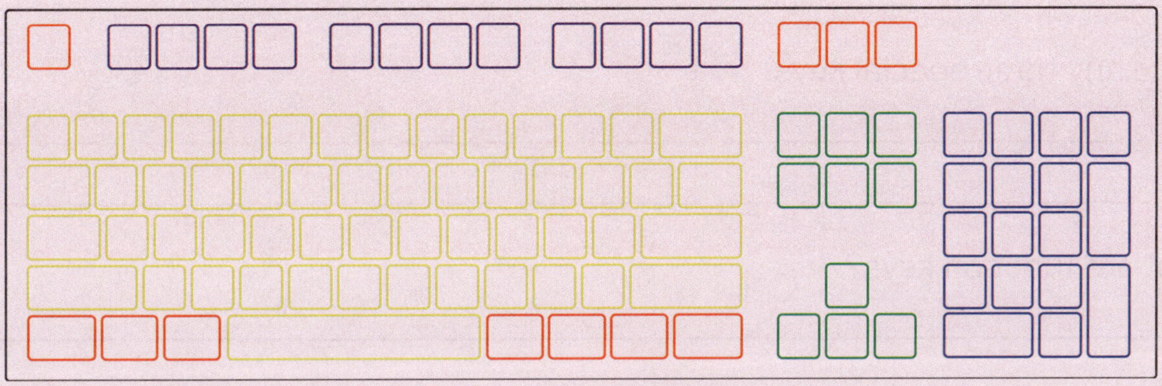

● ______________ ● ______________

● ______________ ● ______________

● ______________

3 Who am I?

a. I am the device used to type data into a computer. ______________

b. I am the key used to type symbols on the number keys. ______________

c. I am the longest key on the keyboard. ______________

d. I am the key that deletes the character to the left of the cursor. ______________

e. I am the key that deletes the character to the right of the cursor. ______________

4. **Answer the following questions.**

a. Write a few lines about the keyboard.

____

____

b. Name the different groups of keys on a keyboard.

____

____

c. How is Backspace key different from Delete key?

____

____

d. Name any three special keys.

____

____

e. What are function keys?

____

____

Mouse—an Input Device

5

What I shall learn

- How to hold and move the mouse
- Point, click and drag using a mouse
- Use the scroll wheel of the mouse

A mouse is a hand-held input device. It is used to point at objects on a computer screen. It is also used to move, open and perform other actions.

Word Web

hand-held: made to be held in the hand

We have already studied that a mouse should always be placed on the mouse pad.

Also, when we move the mouse on the mouse pad, we see a small slanted arrow, called the mouse pointer, moving on the screen. This helps in pointing and selecting the things on the monitor.

Using the Mouse

It is important to hold and move the mouse in the right way. This prevents strain on your wrist, arm and shoulder.

Your arm should be bent at the elbow. You should be able to reach the mouse without extending your arm.

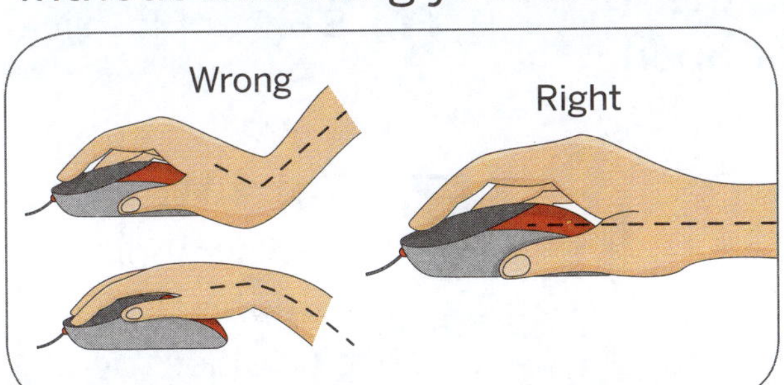

Fig. 5.1 Right way of holding the mouse

Fig. 5.2 Position of the arms while using the mouse

Pointing

When we point at an item on the screen, a small box appears that describes the item. This information is called the **mouse tip**. For example, when we point at the **Recycle Bin** on the desktop, a box appears with the information: Contains the files and folders that you have deleted.

Fig. 5.3 Mouse pointing at the Recycle Bin

The **pointer** can change depending on what it is pointing at. For example, when we point at a link in a web browser, the pointer changes from an arrow to a hand with a pointing finger.

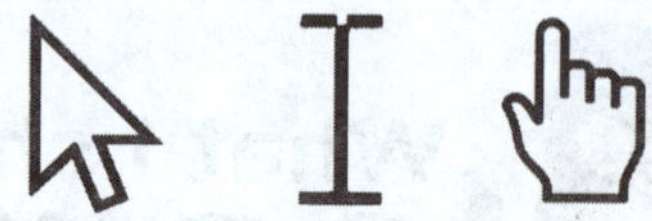

Fig. 5.4 Mouse pointers

Mouse Actions

The left and the right mouse buttons can be clicked. The scroll wheel in the middle allows us to go up or down a page on the monitor. This is called scrolling. Depending on the click, there are four basic actions of mouse buttons: left-click (single-click), double-click, right-click, and drag and drop.

Left-click (Single-click)

To click an item, point at the item on the screen and then, press and release the left button.

Clicking is mostly used to select an item or open a menu. This is sometimes called single-clicking or left-clicking.

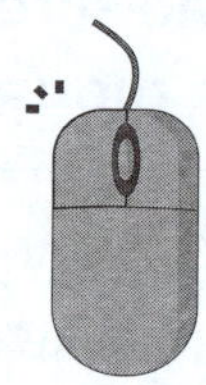

Fig. 5.5 Left-click

Double-click

To double-click an item, point at the item on the screen and then, click twice quickly.

Double-clicking is mostly used to open items on the desktop. For example, we can start a program or open a folder by double-clicking its icon on the desktop.

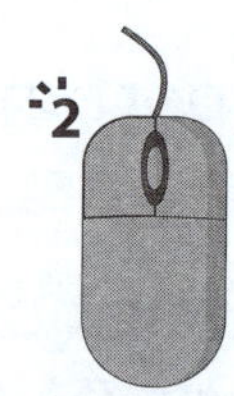

Fig. 5.6 Double-click

Right-click

To right-click an item, point at the item on the screen and then, press and release the right button.

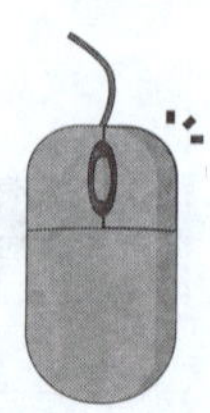

Fig. 5.7 Right-click

Word Web

icon: a symbol that represents a specific object on a desktop

Right-clicking an item displays a list of things we can do with the item. For example, when we right-click the **Recycle Bin** on the desktop, we see a menu with options to open it, empty it, rename it and see its properties. This menu is known as the **Shortcut Menu**.

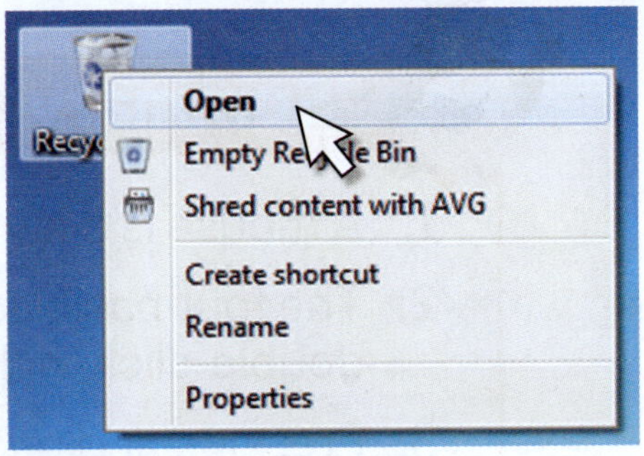

Fig. 5.8 Shortcut menu

Drag and Drop

We can move items around the screen by dragging and dropping them.

To drag an item, point at the item on the screen, press and hold the left-click, and move the item to a new location.

To drop the item, release the left-click.

Drag and drop is mostly used to move files and folders to a different location, and icons around the screen using the mouse.

Using Scroll Wheel

The scroll wheel in a mouse can be used to scroll through documents and web pages.

To scroll down, roll the wheel backward (towards you).

To scroll up, roll the wheel forward (away from you).

Flipping the right and left button of the mouse as per requirement

Microsoft Windows users who are left handers can change the properties of their mouse buttons by following the steps below:

1. On the Windows 8 Start screen or in the Windows 10 search field on the Taskbar, type mouse.
2. Select the change your mouse settings option in the search results.
3. In the Settings window, under Select your primary button, change the selected option in the drop-down list from Left to Right or Right to Left.

Summary

1. A mouse is a hand-held input device.
2. The four basic actions of mouse buttons are left-click (single-click), double-click, right-click, and drag and drop.
3. Pressing and releasing the left mouse button once is called single-click.
4. If the left mouse button is pressed and released twice continuously, it is called double-click.
5. Pressing and holding the left-click button and moving the mouse is called dragging.
6. We can move up and down a screen using the scroll wheel in the mouse.

Teacher's Notes

- Revise the Class 1 chapter on mouse.
- Discuss the different parts of the mouse (left button, right button and scroll wheel).
- Demonstrate the various mouse actions like pointing, clicking, and dragging and dropping.
- Discuss some of the tips to use a mouse properly.

Exercise

1 Fill in the blanks.

a. A mouse is a hand-held ______________ device.

b. ______________ at an item on the screen displays a box with information about the item.

c. ______________ is mostly used to select an item or open a menu.

d. We can move items around the screen by ______________ them.

e. ______________ is used to move the page up and down.

2 Who am I?

a. I am the mouse button used for left-click. ______________

b. I am the mouse button used for right-click. ______________

c. I change depending on what you're pointing at. ______________

d. I am the click used to open items on the desktop. ______________

e. I am the wheel used to move up and down a screen. ______________

3 State whether the following statements are true (T) or false (F).

a. Left-click is done to select an item on the screen. ☐

b. Double-click shows the shortcut menu for the selected item. ☐

c. Right-click opens the file on the screen. ☐

d. Drag and drop is used to move files and folders to a different location. ☐

e. The mouse pointer can change depending on what it is pointing at. ☐

4 Answer the following questions.

a. What is pointing?

____

____

b. List the four ways of using mouse buttons.

____

____

c. What are the functions of single-click and double-click?

____

____

d. What is mouse tip?

____

____

e. Draw any three mouse pointers.

40

Introduction to Paint

6

What I shall learn

- Introduction to Paint software
- Mnimising, maximising and closing Paint window
- Saving the file
- Opening new or the existing file
- Shape tools

Introduction to Paint

We can use a computer to draw and colour pictures.

We use a program called **Microsoft Paint**. It is commonly referred to as **MS Paint** or just **Paint**.

Let us study how we can use this program.

Starting Paint

Follow these steps to start the Paint program.

Word-Web

referred: meant

Step 1:

Click on the **Start** button on the bottom left corner of the screen. The **Start Menu** opens.

Step 2:

Click on **All Programs**.

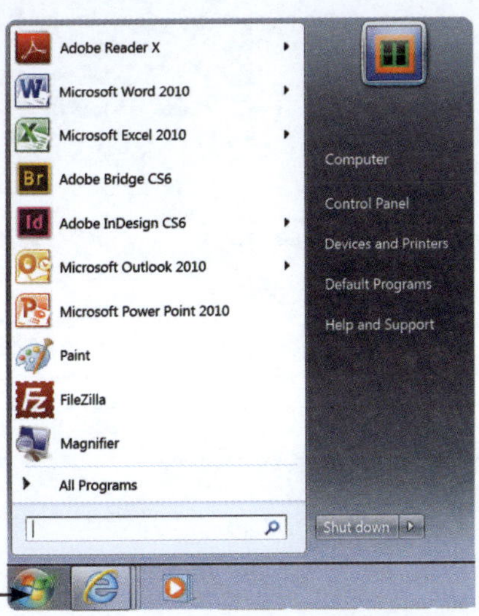

Click on **Start** button.

Fig. 6.1 Click the Start button

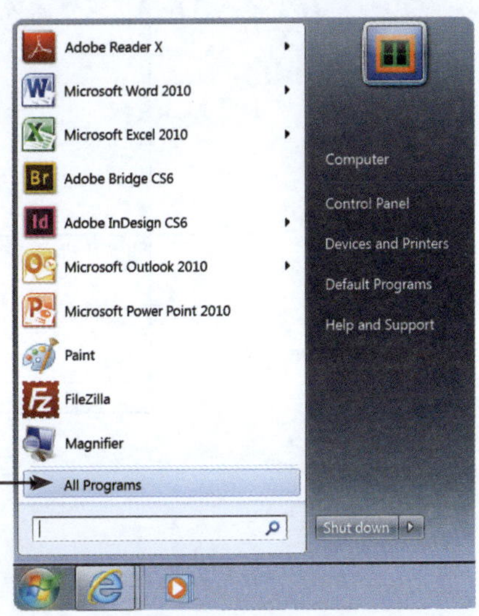

Click on **All Programs.**

Fig. 6.2 Click All Programs

Step 3:

Click on **Accessories**.

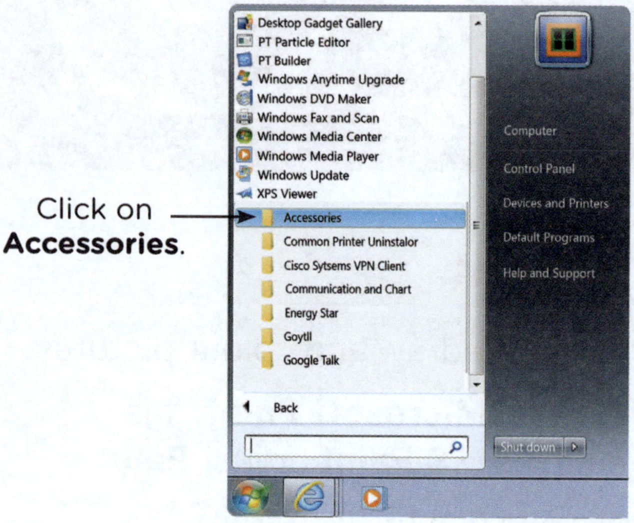

Fig. 6.3 Click Accessories

Step 4:

Click on **Paint** to open the Paint window.

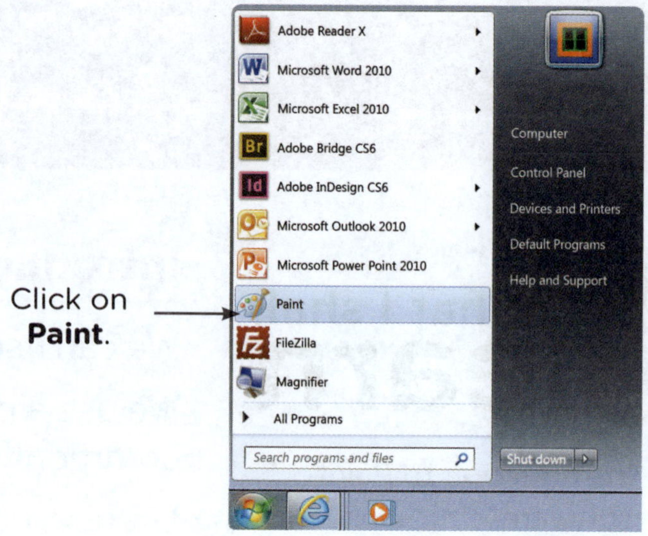

Fig. 6.4 Click Paint

Components of MS Paint Window

The Paint window opens with the **Home** tab selected.

Let us look at some of the important components of the Paint window.

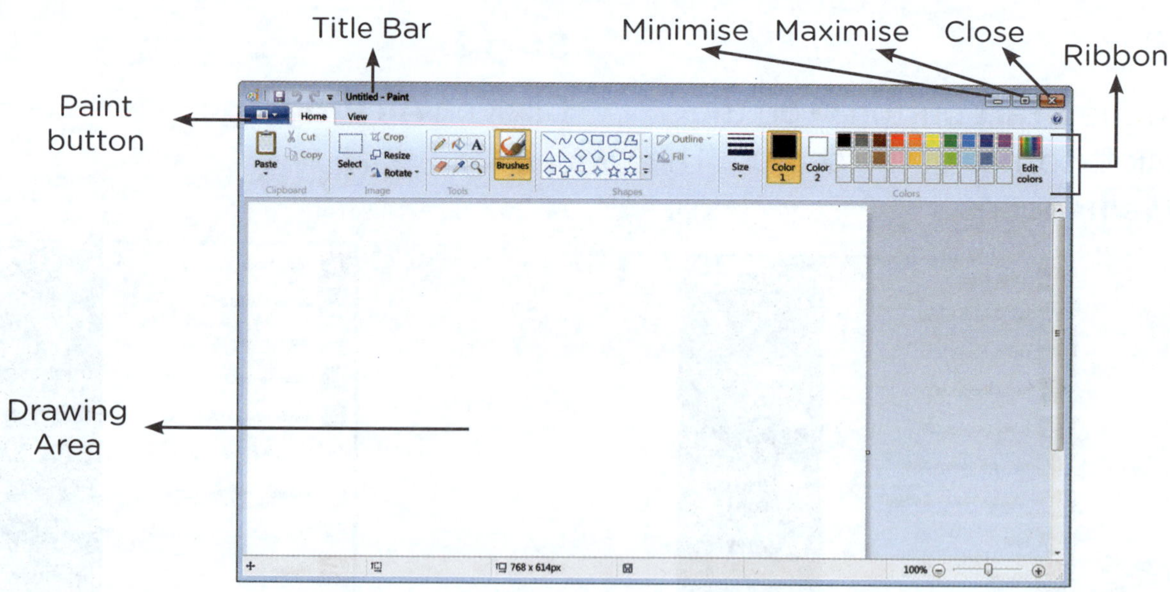

Fig. 6.5 Components of the Paint window

1. Title Bar

This is the bar at the top of the Paint window.

It shows the name of the program (Paint) and the file name.

You Should Know

When you open Paint, the name of the file is 'Untitled', until you give it a new name.

2. Drawing Area

This is the big white area which is used for drawing pictures.

3. Paint button

The Paint button opens a menu that contains various options for working on Paint (Fig. 6.6).

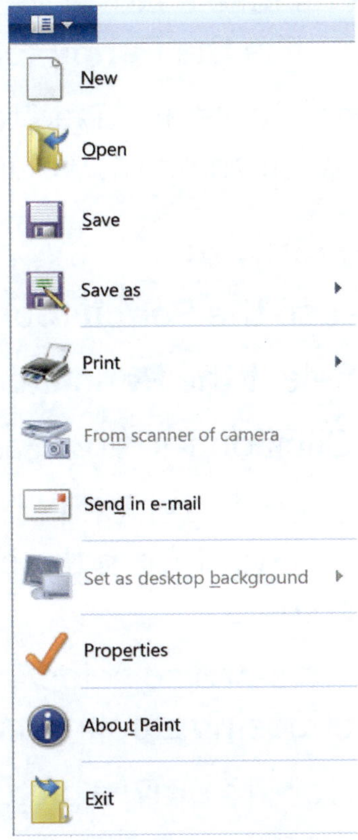

Fig. 6.6 Options after clicking on the Paint button

4. Ribbon

The ribbon contains various tools and commands which help us to draw or paint a picture.

The ribbon contains various **Groups**. Each group has a set of related commands.

5. **Maximise, Minimise and Close button**

At the right-hand end of the Title Bar are the three usual window buttons, Minimise, Maximise and Close.

If your Paint Window is already maximised—taking up all of your screen—the middle button will be Restore, which makes the window the size you usually have it.

- Maximise button will show the full screen. If it is already maximised, in place of Maximise button we get Restore button which in case clicked will make the window smaller.
- Minimise button reduces the current window to a Taskbar button at the bottom. Clicking the button of the Taskbar restores the window to its previous state.
- Close button closes the window.

If it's already maximized, it looks like a box on top of another box. If you click it in that state, it will make your window smaller.

Let us take a closer look at the **Tools** group of buttons which contains various tools like the **Pencil** tool, the **Brushes** tool and many more.

These tools are used to draw pictures in Paint. To choose the colours with which we want to paint, we use the **Colors** group of buttons.

Pencil Tool

We use the **Pencil** tool to draw lines.

1. Select the **Pencil** tool from the **Tools** group.
2. Click on the down arrow below **Size** to select the thickness of the line.
3. Then, to select a colour click on **Color 1** in the **Colors** group. Select the colour you want from the colour palette. This selected colour is called the foreground colour.
4. We can also select a background colour by clicking on **Color 2** and then choosing a colour from the colour palette.
5. Now, to draw a picture, click and drag the mouse inside the **Drawing Area**.

1. Select the **Pencil** tool from the **Tools** group.

2. Click on the arrow below **Size** to select the thickness of the line.

3. Then, to select a colour click on **Color 1** in the **Colors** group. Select the colour you want from the colour palette. This selected colour is called the foreground colour.

4. We can also select a background colour by clicking on **Color 2** and then choosing a colour from the colour palette.

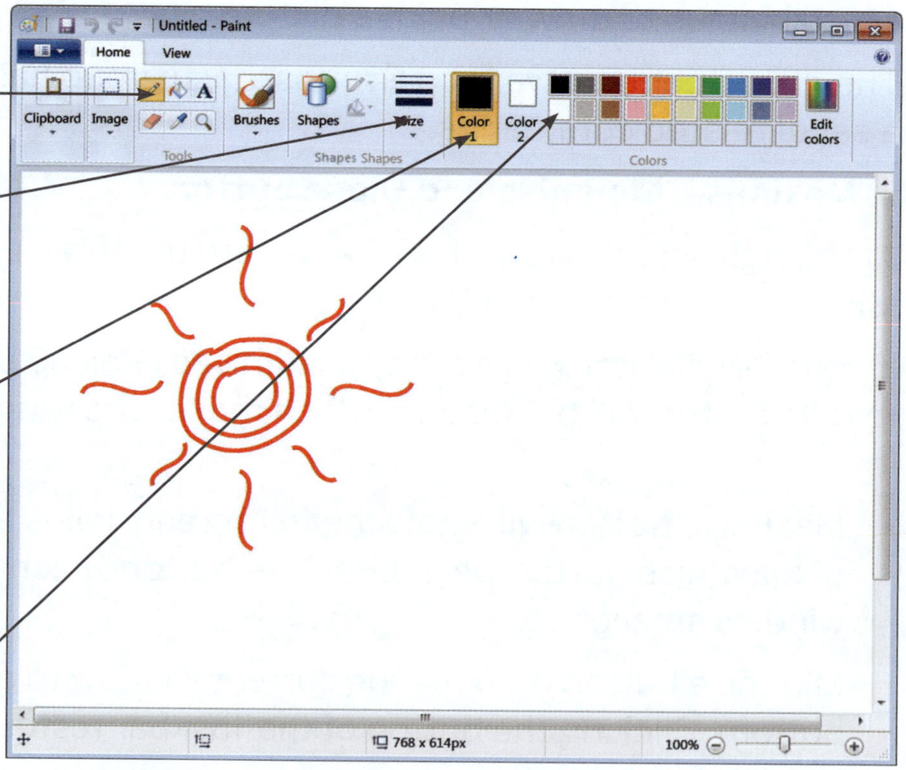

Fig. 6.7 Using the **Pencil** tool

You Should Know

If you want to draw a line using the background colour, right-click on your mouse and then drag it.

Brushes Tool

We use brushes to draw lines and curves. There are different kinds of brushes. They can be used to draw lines of different styles and textures.

1. Select the **Brushes** tool from the **Tools** group. The small arrow under **Brushes** allows us to select different types of brushes.
2. Then, click on the down arrow below **Size** to select the thickness of the brush.
3. Select a foreground colour by clicking on **Color 1** in the **Colors** group.
4. We can also select a background colour by clicking on **Color 2**.
5. To use the brush to paint a picture, click and drag the mouse inside the drawing area.

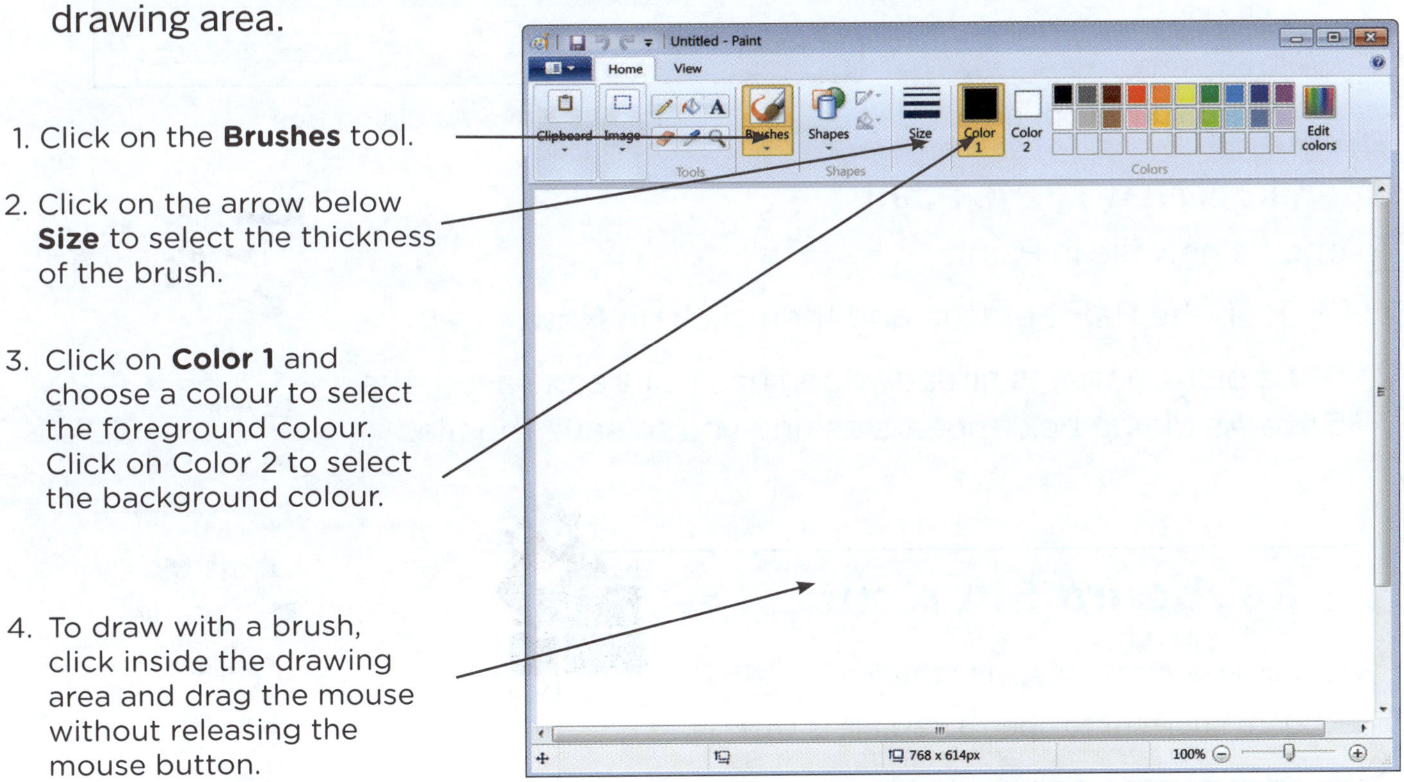

Fig. 6.8 Using the **Brushes** tool

Word-Web

styles: designs

textures: surfaces

Saving Files in Paint

To save a picture drawn in Paint, follow these steps:

1. Click on the **Paint** button and then click on **Save**.
2. In the **Save As** dialog box that appears, give your picture a new name and choose where you want to save the file.
3. Click on the **Save** button.

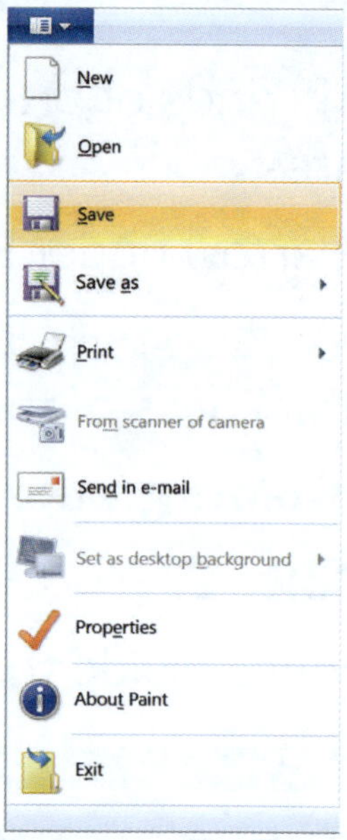

Fig. 6.9 **Save** option

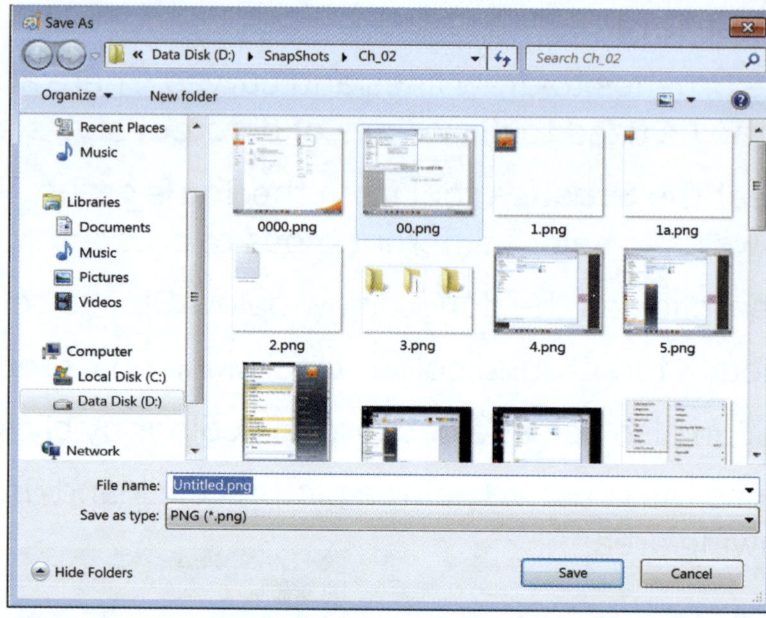

Fig. 6.10 **Save As** dialog box

Opening a New File in Paint

To open a new file in Paint:

1. Click on the **Paint** button and then click on **New**.
2. If the picture that is already open has not been saved, the **Save As** dialog box appears asking you to save the file.

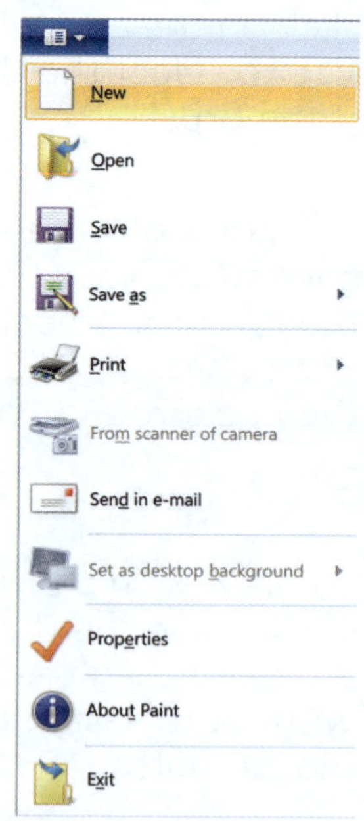

Fig. 6.11 **New** option

Keyboard Shortcuts

Keyboard shortcut for saving the file is **Ctrl+S**.

Keyboard shortcut to open a new file is **Ctrl+N**.

Opening a Previously Saved File in Paint

To open a file that we have previously saved in Paint, follow the steps given below:

1. Click on the **Paint** button and then click on **Open**.

2. The **Open** dialog box opens. Select the drive and the folder where the picture was saved.
3. Now, select the picture you want to open and click on **Open**.

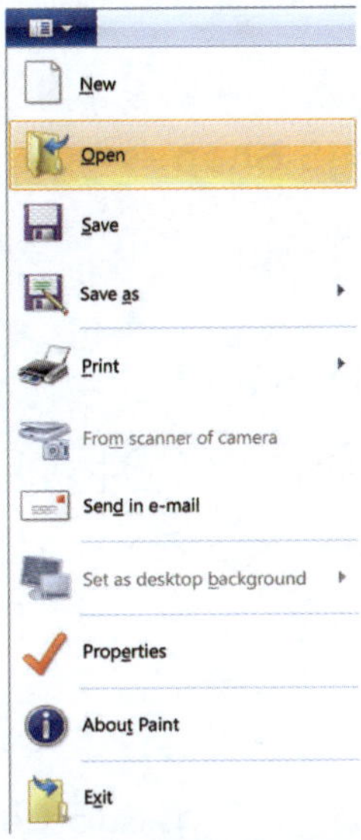

Fig. 6.12 **Open** option

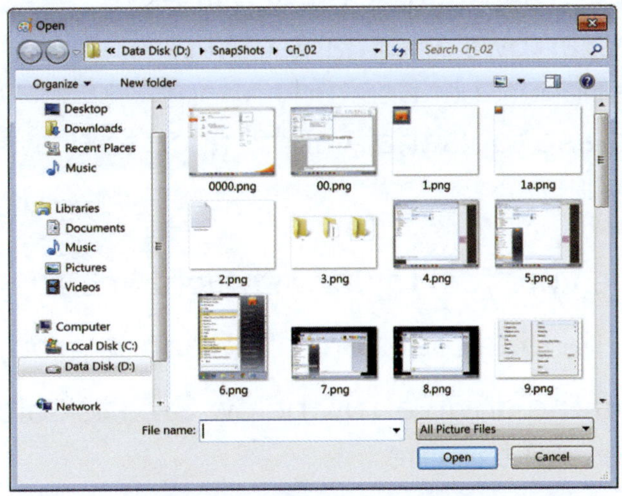

Fig. 6.13 **Open** dialog box

Closing Paint

To close the Paint program, follow the steps given below:

1. Click on the **Paint** button and then click on **Exit**.
2. If the picture that is already open has not been saved, the **Save As** dialog box appears asking you to save the file.

We can also close the Paint program by clicking on the red button with the cross at the top right corner of the Paint window. This is also known as the **Close** button.

Keyboard Shortcuts

Keyboard shortcut to open an existing file is **Ctrl+O** and to close Paint is **Alt+F4**.

Fig. 6.14 **Exit** option

Drawing In Paint

You now know how to start and close Paint, how to open and save files in Paint.

You have also seen how the Paint window looks and the tools we use to draw and colour the pictures.

Let us now look at some more tools that we have in Paint.

Shapes Toolbox

The **Shapes** group contains the **Shapes** toolbox which has many tools that can be used for drawing. These tools allow us to draw straight lines, curved lines, rectangles, arrows and many other different shapes. Let us study about some of these tools that can be used to draw pictures.

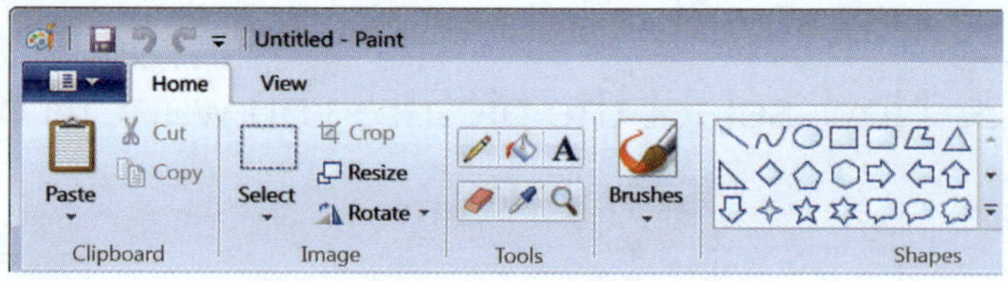

Fig. 6.15 **Shapes** group

Line Tool

We use the **Line** tool to draw straight lines.

1. Select the **Line** tool from the **Shapes** group.
2. Click on the down arrow below **Size** to select the thickness of the line.
3. Now, select a foreground colour by clicking on **Color 1** in the **Colors** group and then choose a colour. You can also select a background colour by clicking on **Color 2** and then choosing a colour.
4. To draw a picture, click and drag the mouse pointer inside the **Drawing Area**.
5. You can also select different styles of lines by clicking on the small downward pointing arrow beside **Outline** button.

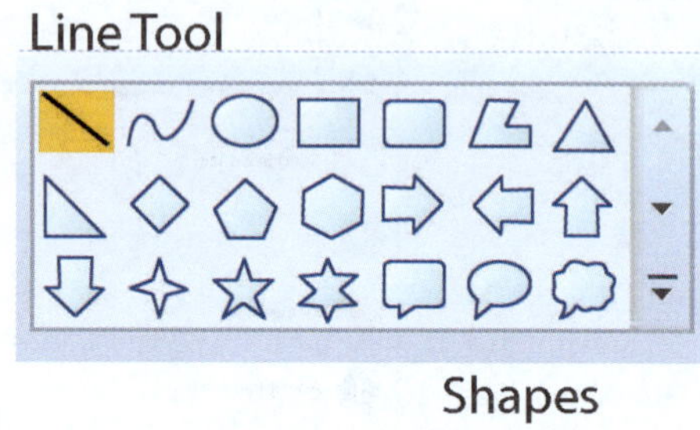

Fig. 6.16 **Line** tool

Outline button

1. Click on the **Line** tool.
2. Click on the arrow below **Size** to select the thickness of the line.
3. Click on **Color 1** and choose a colour to select the foreground colour. Click on **Color 2** to select the background colour.
4. To draw a line, click inside the drawing area and drag the mouse without releasing the mouse button.

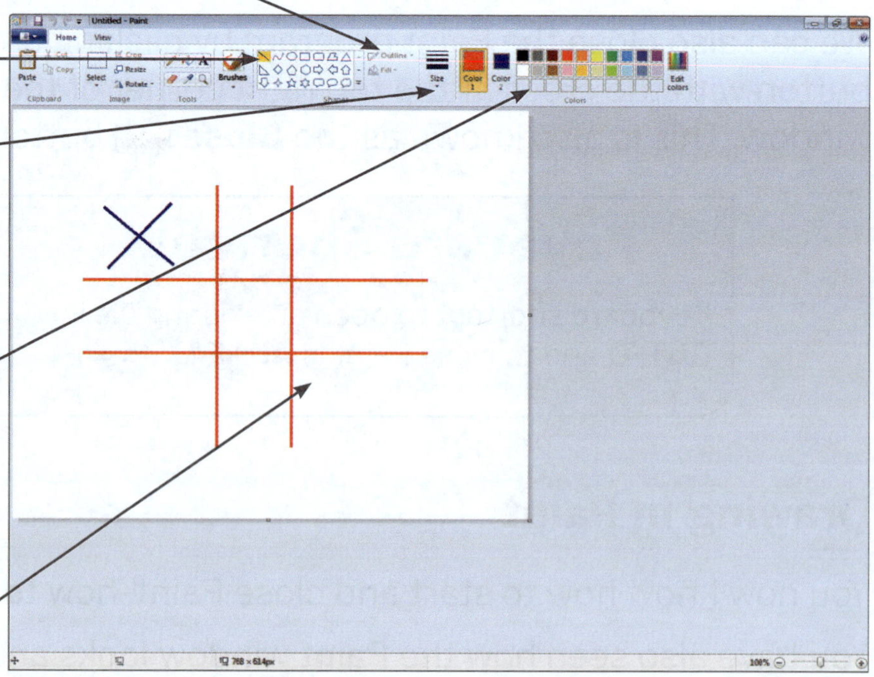

Fig. 6.17 Using the **Line** tool

You Should Know

To draw a line using the background colour, right-click your mouse and then drag it.

Curve Tool

We use the **Curve** tool to draw curved lines.

1. Select the **Curve** tool from the **Shapes** group.
2. Next, select the line thickness and the colour. You can also change the style by clicking the small downward pointing arrow beside **Outline**.
3. Now, click and drag the mouse in the **Drawing Area**. You'll get a straight line. Click the line and then drag it to get a curved line.

Curve Tool

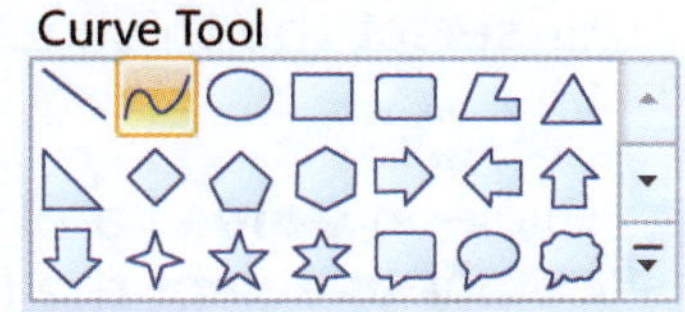

Shapes

Fig. 6.18 **Curve** tool

1. Click on the **Curve** tool.
2. Click on the arrow below **Size** to select the thickness of the line.
3. Click on **Color 1** and choose a colour to select the foreground colour. Click on **Color 2** to select the background colour.
4. Click and drag the mouse to get a straight line. Now, click the line and then drag it to get a curved line.

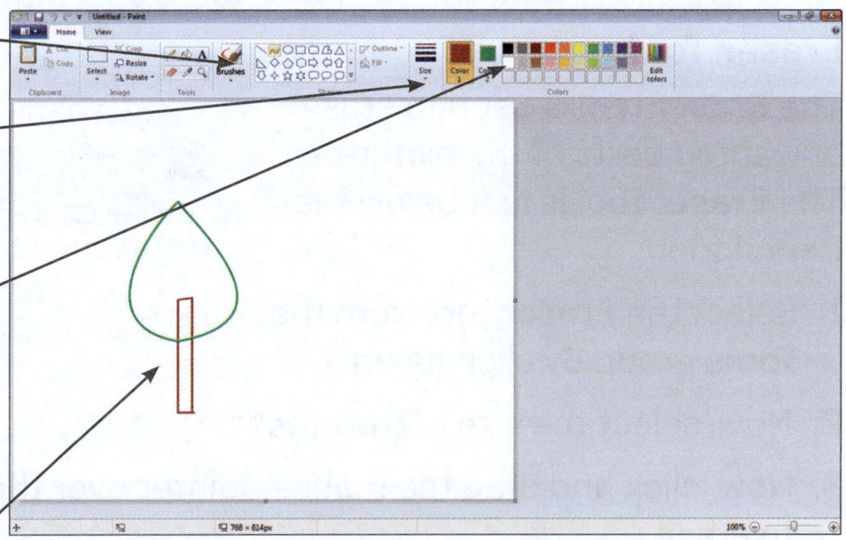

Fig. 6.19 Using the **Curve** tool

Polygon Tool

We use the **Polygon** tool to draw shapes with many sides.

1. Select the **Polygon** tool from the **Shapes** group.
2. To draw the polygon, click and drag the mouse to draw a straight line.

Polygon Tool

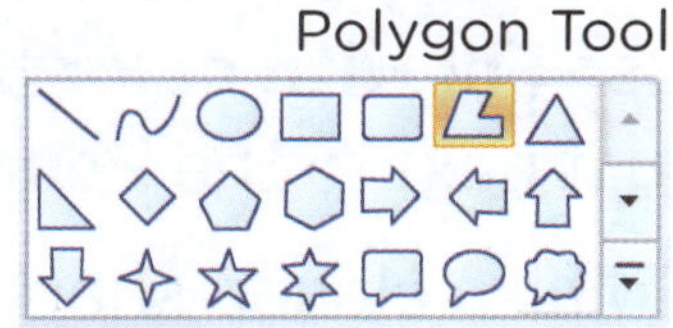

Shapes

Fig. 6.20 **Polygon** tool

3. Now, click on each point where you want the tip of the polygon to appear.
4. Finish the polygon by clicking on a point on the polygon and closing the shape.

1. Click on the **Polygon** tool.
2. Click on the arrow below **Size** to select the thickness of the line.
3. Click on **Color 1** and choose a colour to select the foreground colour. Click on **Color 2** to select the background colour.
4. Click and drag the mouse to draw the shape by connecting the lines and the points.

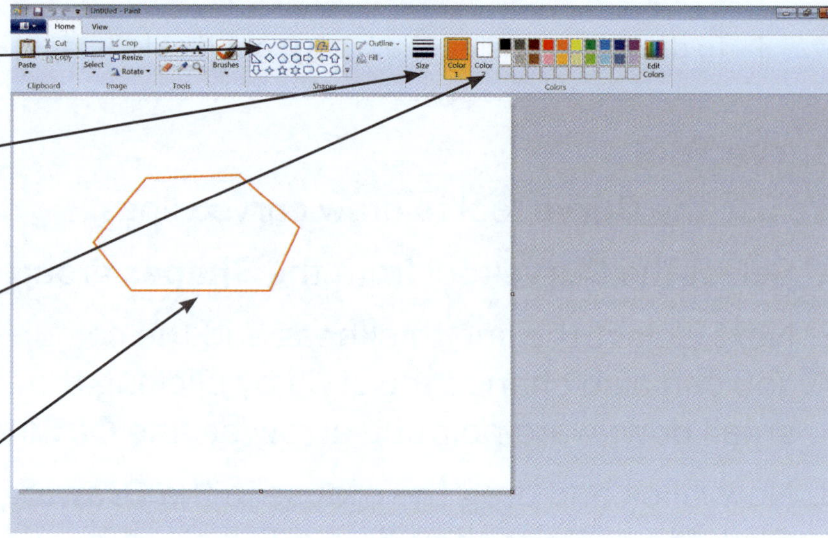

Fig. 6.21 Using the **Polygon** tool

Eraser Tool

The **Eraser** tool is used to erase unwanted parts of the picture. The **Eraser** tool is just below the **Pencil** tool.

Eraser Tool

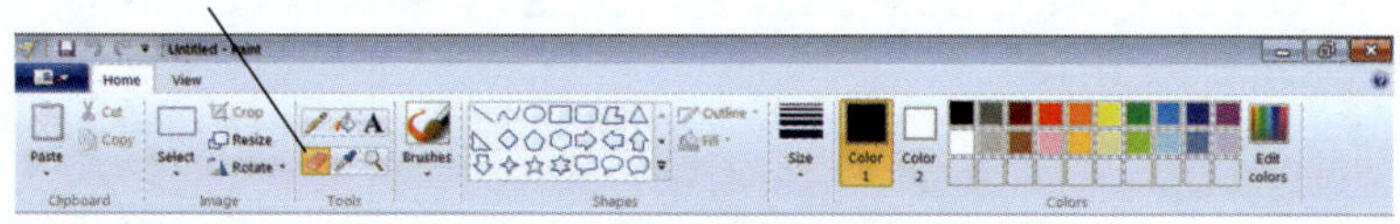

Fig. 6.22 **Eraser** tool

1. Select the **Eraser** tool from the **Tools** group by clicking on it.
2. Now, select the size of the eraser.
3. Now, click and drag the mouse pointer over the parts of the image you want to erase.

Fill with Color Tool

To fill any closed shape with the selected colour use **Fill with color** tool. It is in the **Tools** group, just next to the **Pencil** tool.

Fill with Color Tool

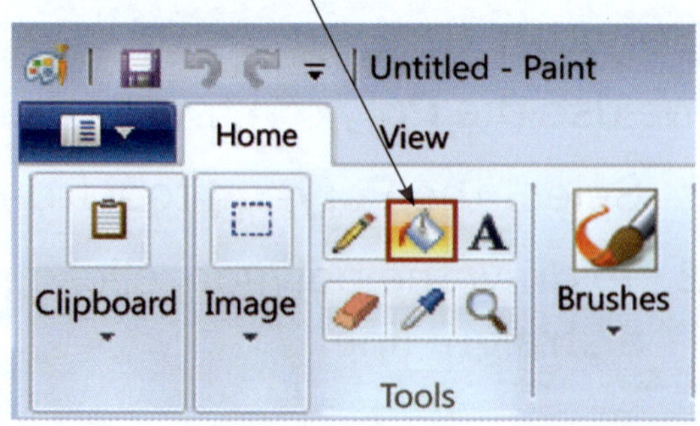

Fig. 6.23 Using the **Fill with color**

To fill a closed shape with a selected colour:

1. Choose the **Fill with color** tool from the **Tools** group.
2. Select the colour you want to use after clicking on **Color 1**.
3. Click inside the shape you want to fill with colour.

Text Tool

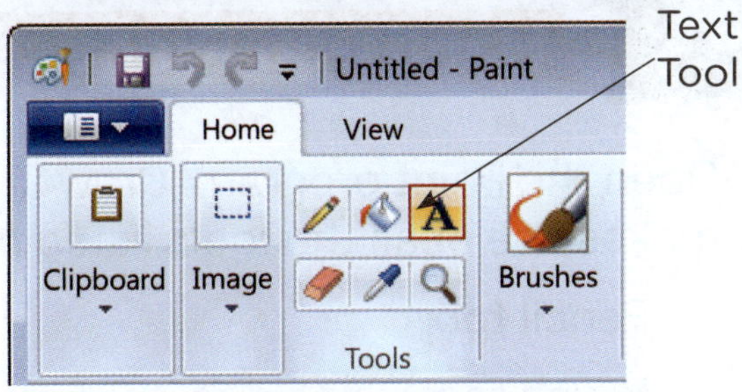

Fig. 6.24 **Text** tool

To write in the drawing area in Paint, we use the **Text** tool.

This tool is in the **Tools** group, just next to the **Fill with color** tool.

1. To select the **Text** tool, click on it.
2. Click in the drawing area where you want to enter the text. The cursor appears on the screen.
3. The **Text** tab is automatically selected instead of the **Home** tab. Select the font size and style in the **Font** group.
4. Now, select the colour of the text by clicking on **Color 1** and then selecting a colour.
5. Use your keyboard to type the text.

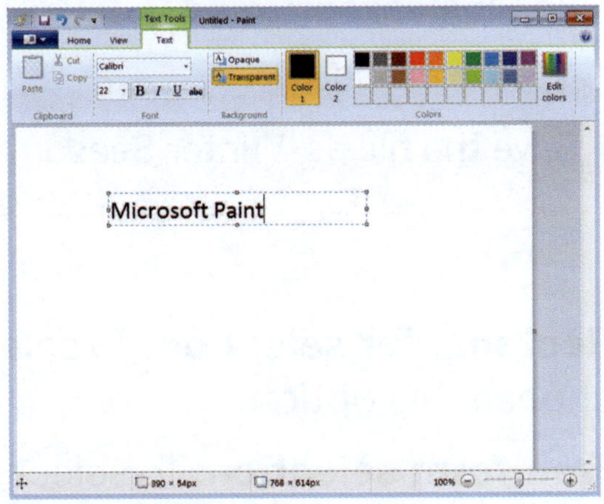

Fig. 6.25 Using the **Text** tool

You Should Know

1. **Eraser** tool can also be used to add a background colour while erasing the picture. To do this, select Color 2 after selecting the size of the eraser. Then, select the required colour from the colour palette. Now, right-click and drag the mouse pointer where you want to apply the background colour.
2. If there is any gap in the outline of the shape or if the shape is not closed, the colour may spill to other areas of the picture while using this tool.

Select Tool

To select different parts of the picture, use the **Select** tool.

The Select tool is in the Image group.

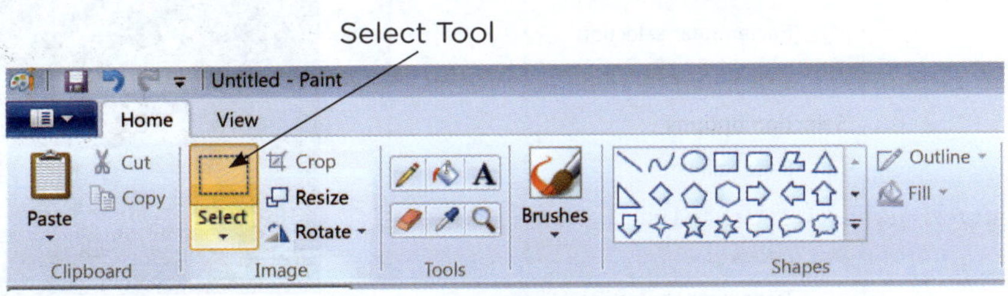

Fig. 6.26 **Select** tool

1. Click the small down arrow under **Select** button to open a menu.
2. You can select different selection shapes from the drop-down menu.

Hands-on Practice

Open the Paint program. Draw a winter season with an igloo house picture that makes use of all the tools listed below:

1. Pencil tool
2. Brush tool
3. Shapes tool
4. Eraser tool etc.

Save the file as 'Winter Season'.

Rectangular selection: To select a square or rectangular area in the picture, choose this option.

Free-form selection: To select an irregular shape, choose this option.

Select all: To select the entire picture, choose this option.

Invert selection: To select everything in the picture apart from what is currently selected, click on this option.

Delete: To delete the selected area of the picture, click on this option.

Word-Web

irregular: unequal

magnify: expand, enlarge

invert: turn upside down

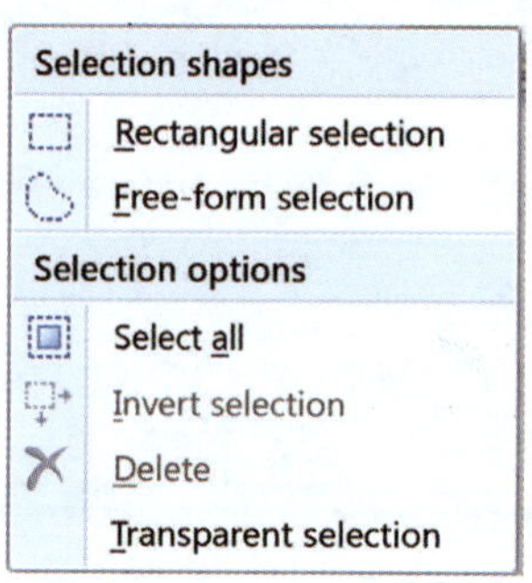

Fig. 6.27 Rectangular selection

Fig. 6.28 Using the **Rectangular selection** tool

Magnifier Tool

Fig. 6.29 **Magnifier** tool

To magnify or zoom in different parts of the picture, we use the **Magnifier** tool.

The **Magnifier** tool is in the **Tools** group, just under the Text tool.

To use this tool:

1. Click on the **Magnifier** tool.
2. Move the mouse on the part of the image you want to magnify. You'll see that the usual mouse pointer is replaced by a big box and a magnifying glass. This big box and a magnifying glass shows which part of the picture is going to be magnified when you use the **Magnifier** tool.

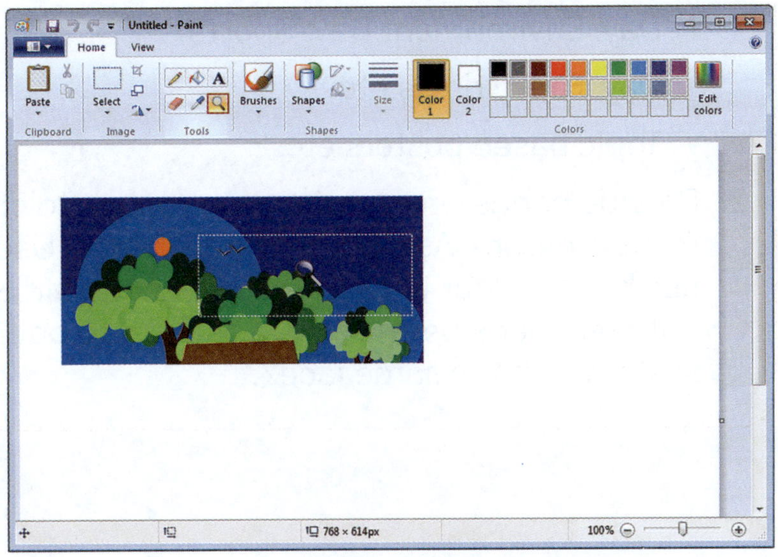

Fig. 6.30 **Magnifier** tool

Summary

1. Paint program is used to draw and colour pictures on the computer.
2. To start Paint click on Start - All Programs - Accessories – Paint.
3. The important components of the Paint window are the Title Bar, Minimise, Maximise and Close button, Drawing Area, Paint button and Ribbon.
4. The Ribbon contains the Groups like the Tools group of buttons, the colors group of buttons and the Shapes group of buttons.
5. To draw lines use tools like Pencils or Brushes.
6. To draw different shapes like polygon, square, oval etc. use the shapes group buttons.
7. To select the foreground colour, click on Color 1 in the Colors group of buttons and then select the colour.
8. To select the background colour, click on Color 2 in the colors group of buttons and then select the colour.
9. To open new or existing files and to save the files, select the required option after clicking the Paint button.
10. To exit from the Paint program, click on the Close button.

Lab Activity

1. Demonstrate some examples of paint activities on the computer such as:
    - Birthday cards
    - Pictures to illustrate Children's
    - Day, Environment Day, Sports
    - Day, Fancy dress etc.
    - Topic based posters etc.
2. Provide hands-on experience in groups to children on the computer to start the Paint program. Ask them to draw a face. Use yellow colour to draw the face. Next use black colour to draw the eyes and hair. Save the file as 'Face'. Close Paint. With teacher's permission, ask them to open the file called 'Face' in their friend's system. Is it the same face?.

Teacher's Notes

- Explain the purpose and usage of the paint software.
- Demonstrate the activities related to opening, minimising, maximising and closing Paint window.
- Demonstrate saving the file at the desired location.
- Demonstrate opening/editing the existing file.
- Show shape tools to draw pictures.

Exercise

1 Fill in the blanks

a. Using Microsoft Paint program we can ______________ and ______________.

b. To open Paint program: Start ▶ ______________ ▶ Accessories ▶ ______________.

c. ______________ toolbox contains many tools that can be used for drawings.

d. Eraser tool can be used to erase ______________ parts.

e. ______________ tool is used to write in the drawing area in Paint.

2 State whether the following statements are true (T) or false (F).

a. To open a file that we have saved previously in Paint, we use save command. [ ]

b. We close the Paint program using exit button. [ ]

c. Eraser tool is present just below the Pencil tool. [ ]

d. We use line tool to draw a curve line. [ ]

e. Free-form selection tool helps to select an irregular shape. [ ]

3 Answer the following questions:

a. State the uses of an Eraser tool.

____

____

____

b. Is it possible to insert text in a drawing? If yes, how?

____

____

____

c. How can we draw a shape with many sides?

____

____

____

d. Name the different components of a Paint window.

____

____

____

e. How is Color 1 option is different from Color 2 option?

____

____

____

4 **Label the parts of the MS Paint window that you've studied in this chapter.**

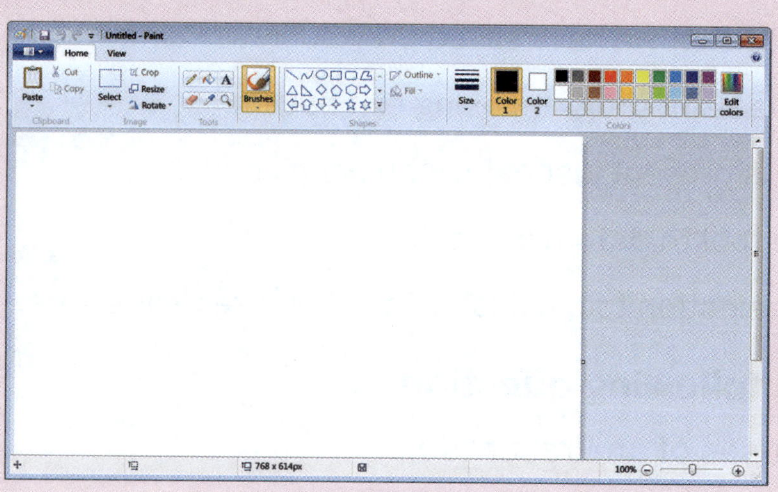

File Management

7

What I shall learn

- Concept of saving a file and its purpose
- Saving a file in the specified path

File Management

A computer has many programs (applications). These programs have many files.

A **file** is an item that contains information like text or images or music. When opened, a file can look like a text document or a picture that we might find on someone's desk. Files are represented with icons on a computer. This makes it easy to recognize a type of file by looking at its icon. Some common file icons are given in Fig. 7.1.

① Contact ② Picture ③ Text document

Fig. 7.1 Common file icons

A **folder** is a container where we can store files. If we have thousands of paper files on our desk, it will be nearly impossible to find the file we need. That's why people often store paper files in folders. On our computer, folders work in the same way.

Some common folder icons are given in Fig. 7.2.

Folders can also store other folders. A folder within a folder is usually called a **subfolder**. We can create any number of subfolders and each can hold any number of files and additional subfolders.

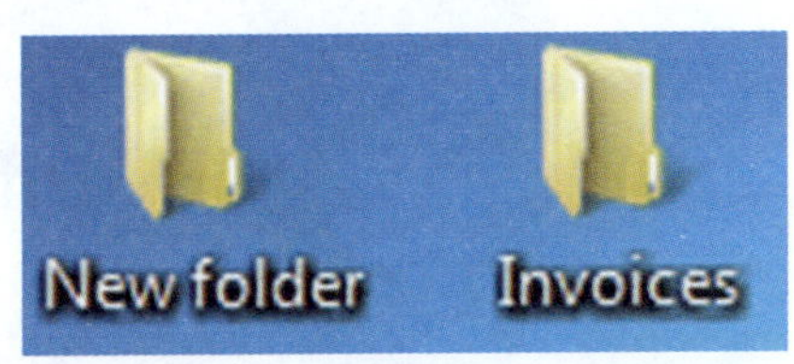

(a) (b)

Fig. 7.2 (a) An empty folder (b) A folder containing files

Save

Save is the process of writing data to storage devices like floppy disk, CD, pen drive or hard disk.

Fig. 7.3: Save Icons

The save icon typically looks like a floppy disk.

Saving a file using Save and Save as commands

You can use the **Save** and **Save As** commands to store your work, and you can adjust the settings that an application uses to save your files.

For example, if the document is for your own use and you never expect to open it in an older version of application, you can use the **Save** command.

If you want to share your document with people who use different version, or if you plan to open the file on another computer, you need to choose how and where you want to save the document.

Save a document for the first time

On the **Quick Access Toolbar**, click **Save**  or press CTRL+S.

Type a name for the document, and then click **Save**.

This saves the file in a default location.

To save the document in a different location,

a. Click **This PC**.

b. Select the files or folders using the navigation in the left-hand side to which you want to save the file.

c. Type a name for the file then click **Save**.

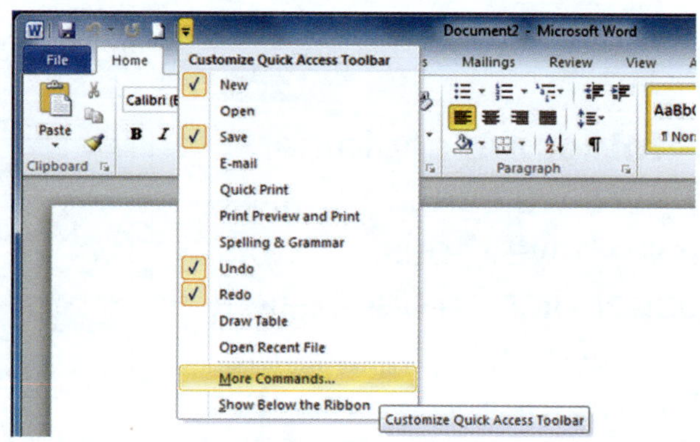

Fig. 7.4 Save option in Quick Access Toolbar

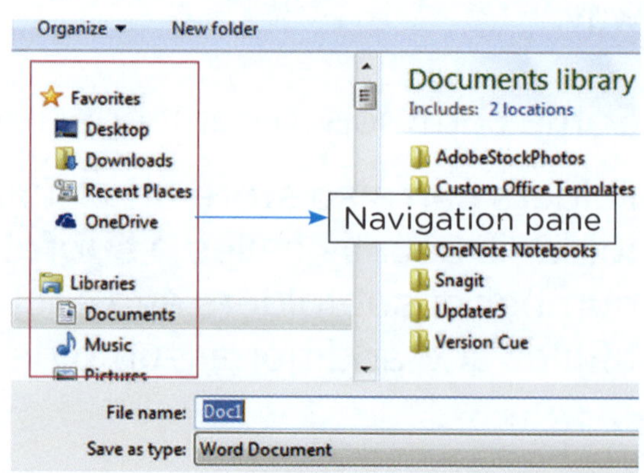

Fig. 7.5 Select path to save a file

Word Web

icon: small pictures

typically: normally

navigation: routing

Save an existing document as a new document (Save As)

To prevent overwriting the original file, use the **Save As** command to create a new file as soon as you open the original document.

1. Open the file that you want to save as a new file.
2. Click the **File** tab.
3. Click **Save As**.
4. Type a name for the document, and then click **Save**.

To save the document in a different location, click another folder in the **Save in** list in the **Save As** dialog box.

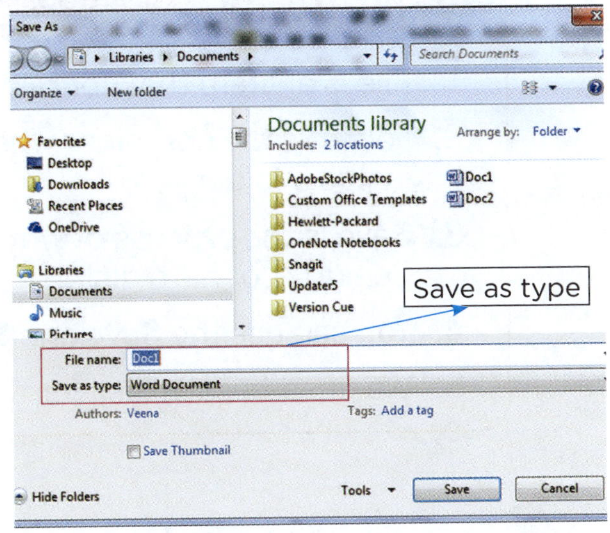

Fig. 7.6 Save As

Why do we need to save files?

Unless the program you are using automatically saves, as you are working, if a file is not saved it is lost. For example, if you are writing a book and power to your computer is lost, or the computer crashes, anything that was typed written that was not saved is lost.

Word Web

default: already specified

overwrite: write on top of

crash: failure

Hands-on Practice

Open Notepad. Write down a paragraph of five-six sentences about computers. Now, save the file as Computers and exit Notepad.

Now, give a title to the paragraph you wrote. Open Notepad again and open the file Computers.

Then, give the title 'Computers in Our Live'.

Save the file as 'Computers in Our Lives' on Desktop without overwriting the file 'Computers'.

Summary

1. File is an item that contains an image, text, sound or videos etc.
2. Folder is the container where files are stored. Subfolder is the folder stored inside a folder.
3. Save is the process of writing data to storage devices like floppy disk, CD, pen drive or hard disk.
4. You can use the Save and Save As commands to store your work.
5. We need to save files for the future use without losing it.

Lab Activity

Visit your lab. Open Notepad. Write a paragraph about your Home. Save your file as 'My Home' and close the window. Open Notepad again and open the file 'My Home'. Write one more paragraph about it. Now, save the file as 'My Sweet Home' and save in the desired location.

Teacher's Notes

- Explain the concept of a file and the need for saving it.
- Conduct hands-on activities (individual or group) like 'Treasure Hunt' where a child will locate the file saved by her/his friend on the Computer to learn the concept of saving the files in any desired location.

Exercise

1 Fill in the blanks

a. The shortcut key for saving files is ______________.

b. Folder can store ______________ and ______________.

c. To prevent overwriting the original file, use the ______________ command.

d. A computer has many ______________.

e. We can save file using ______________ and ______________ commands in the File tab.

2 State whether the following statements are true (T) or false (F).

a. Files can store folders into it. ☐

b. We need not save files using the commands Save and Save As. ☐

c. We can overwrite a file without changing the original file. ☐

d. Folders can store subfolders. ☐

e. Files can be saved in the storage devices like CD, Pen drive, Hard disk etc. ☐

3 Answer the following questions.

a. Define the terms file, folder and sub-folder.

____

____

____

b. What is Save?

____

____

____

c. Why do we need to save a file?

____

____

____

d. How can we save a file for the first time?

____

____

____

e. Write the keyboard shortcut for saving a file.

____

____

____

Worksheet 1

Chapters 1–3

1 Identify the following places where the computers are being used and write about the usage.

a. 

A__M M__c__in__

It is used for

____

b. 

In S__h__ __l

It is used to

____

c. 

In Ra__l__a__ St__ti__n

It is used to

____

d. 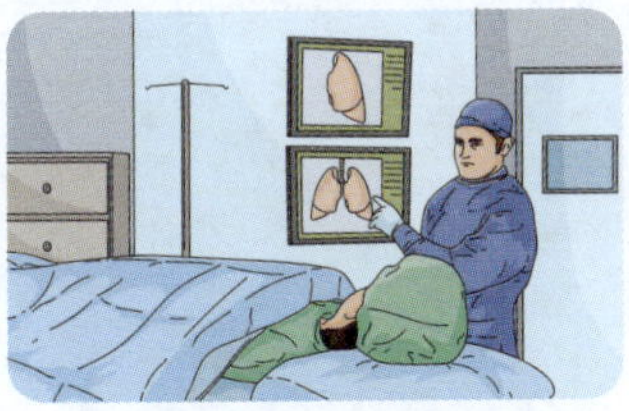

In H__sp__t__l

It is used to

____

e 

At__o__ __

It is used to

____

❷ Write two lines about each of the following.

a. Computer - An Electronic Machine

____

____

b. Storage Devices

____

____

c. Digital Camera

____

____

d. Monitor

____

____

e. ALU

____

____

Worksheet 2

Chapters 4–7

1 Unscramble the given words to fill in the blanks.

1. We can draw and colour images using ________________ (CRMOFSIOT TIPAN)
2. We can open Paint application using Start button ________________. (SOACECSRISE)
3. ________________ is the big white area which is used for drawing pictures in MS Paint. (WDIGRAN EARA)
4. The ________________ contains various tools and commands which help us to draw or paint a picture. (ONRBIB)
5. The ________________ opens a menu that contains various options for working on Paint. (INAPT ONTBUT)

2 Match the following.

a. 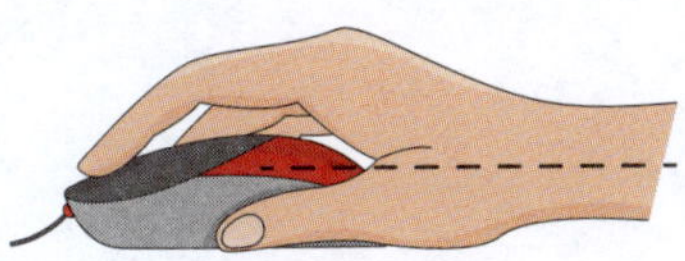

i. Left button of a mouse

b. 

ii. Keyboard

c. 

iii. Mouse tip

d. 

iv. Num pad

e. 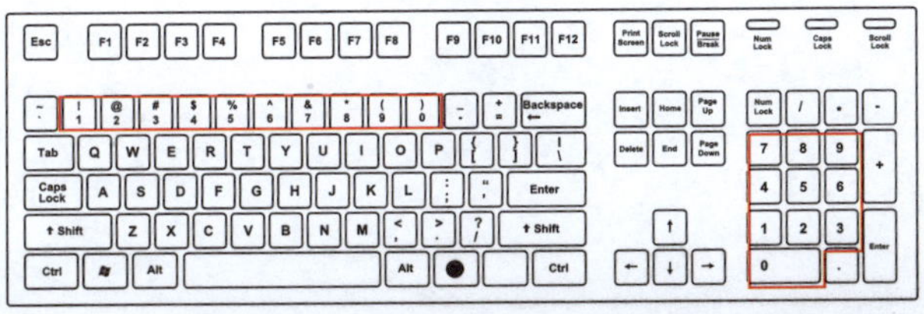

v. Escape key

❸ **Identify and name the labelled parts of the given keyboard.**

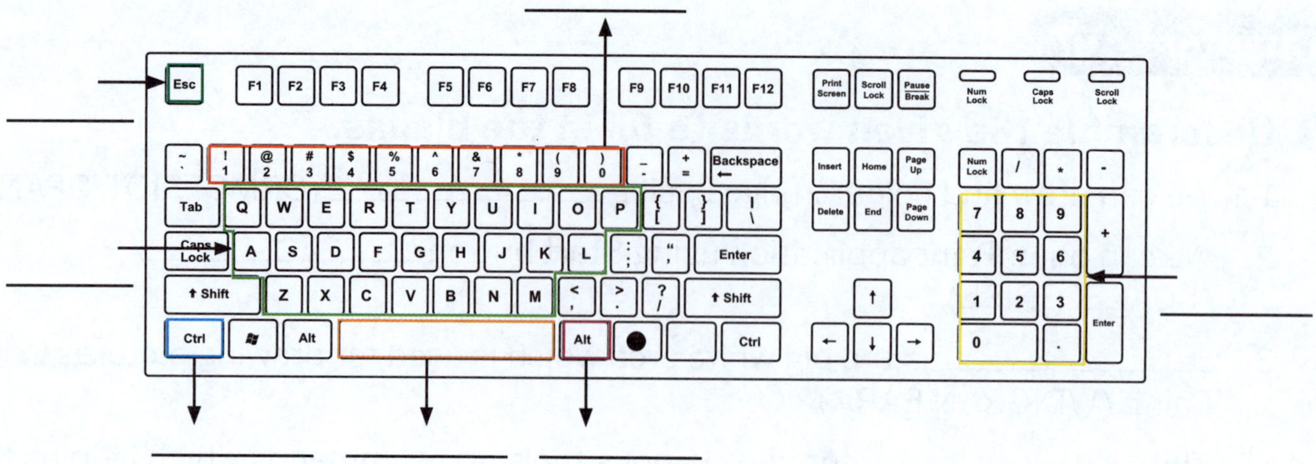

Projects

a. Draw a mouse and colour it (show the variation among the three buttons in colouring). Mark the parts of the mouse and write few sentences about the mouse actions and also the uses of mouse.

b. Click pictures using your camera whenever you see the computers are being used by the people in different places apart from the lesson topics. Stick those photographs in a scrapbook and write a few lines about them.

c. Create a park scene using the MS Paint software and stick the printout in a scrapbook.

Assessment 1

Chapters 1–3 **(Maximum Marks: 20)**

1 **Explain a scenario with the appropriate pictures for the Input-Process-Output cycle.** **(5 marks)**

2 **Write a few lines about each of the following devices.** **(10 marks)**

a. Keyboard

b. Web Camera

c. Printer

d. Smart card

e. Scanner

3. **Write the advantages and disadvantages of using the computers.** **(5 marks)**

Advantages

Disadvantages

Assessment 2

Chapters 4–7 **(Maximum Marks: 20)**

1 Fill in the blanks. (5 marks)

a. ________________ in MS Paint has Polygon tool, Curve tool, etc.

b. The key that is used to give space between characters is ________________ key.

c. Ctrl, Esc and Alt are called as ________________ keys.

d. ________________ is the mouse action most often used to open items on your desktop.

e. We can move items around the screen of the computer by ________________ them.

2 State whether the following statements are true (T) or false (F). (5 marks)

a. We can use Backspace to scroll through documents up and down. ☐

b. An indicator at the top of the keyboard or on the 'Num Lock' key shows that it is on or not. ☐

c. Alternate is the full form of Alt key. ☐

d. If we hold down Ctrl key and type letters we get uppercase letters on the screen. ☐

e. Left click is the mouse action most often used to select an item. ☐

3 Answer the following questions. (10 marks)

a. How can we flip the right mouse button to the left mouse button and vice-versa?

____

b. How many alphabet keys do you have in your keyboard at home?

____

c. Name the three buttons of mouse.

____

d. What is mouse tip?

____

e. Explain drag and drop action.

____

Revision Questions

1. **Fill in the blanks.**
   a. We use the ____________________ to draw shapes with many sides in MS Paint.
   b. We use the ____________________ to draw lines in MS Paint.
   c. ____________________ option will select everything in the picture apart from what is currently selected.
   d. The ____________________ contains buttons for basic commands, saving and printing.
   e. The ____________________ contains the name of the file or application.

2. **State whether the following statements are true (T) or false (F).**
   a. A computer can cook in the kitchen. ☐
   b. QWERTY keyboard is used by the blind person to type. ☐
   c. Fill with Color tool is in the Tools group, just next to the Pencil tool. ☐
   d. When the computer crashes, anything that was typed is lost. ☐
   e. To save an existing document as a new document, we use Ctrl + S command. ☐

3. **Answer the following questions briefly.**
   a. What is dragging?
   ____
   ____
   b. Write the full form of Esc and Ctrl.
   ____
   ____
   c. In your school, do teachers use computers? If yes, what is the purpose?
   ____
   ____
   d. Why do people use computer at home?
   ____
   ____

e. What is the extension of the MS Paint file?

____

____

4. Answer the following questions in detail.

a. What is a file?

____

____

b. Write the various advantages of a computer.

____

____

c. State the uses of numeric keypad.

____

____

d. Name the five parts of MS Paint window.

____

____

e. Which is the drawing area in MS Paint window?

____

____

Computer Manners

Always follow the instructions of your computer teacher in the lab.

1. Do not sit too close to the computer screen. It may harm your eyes.

2. Always use a mouse pad for the mouse.

3. Do not take a magnet near a computer.

4. Do not push the computer table. Some part may fall and get damaged.

Introduction to Tux Typing

Tux Typing is a fun-filled educational typing program that helps to improve the typing skills. Although, it is made for young children but it can also be used by adults. You can learn typing through a number of games starring the **Tux Penguin Mascot**. The games can be played at three difficulty levels – Easy, Medium and Hard.

Features of Tux Typing

Tux Typing is designed to be an exciting and educational software application to improve typing speed. The various features of Tux Typing are as follows:

1. It is a free typing tutor program created for children.
2. It is available for Windows, Linux and Mac operating systems.
3. It supports various languages like English, Spanish, German, French, Japanese, Hindi, etc.
4. The fun sounds in Tux Typing makes gaming all the more interesting.
5. It can be freely downloaded from http://tux4kids.alioth.debian.org/tuxtype/download.php
6. It also contains finger lessons on various keys on the keyboard.

You already know that to gain expertise in typing, you need to look at the screen while typing and practice often to get used to the positioning of the keys on the keyboard. Before we go ahead, let us recapitulate the correct way of typing using the keyboard.

You Should Know

The typing speed is measured in words per minute (wpm).

The picture given below shows the ideal position of your fingers on the keyboard.

Left hand positioning: Finger 1 of left hand should be placed on the letter A, finger 2 on the letter S, finger 3 on letter D, finger 4 on letter F and the thumb of left hand (numbered as 5) should be on the Spacebar.

Right hand positioning: The thumb of right hand (numbered as 6) should be placed on the Spacebar, finger 7 on the letter J, finger 8 on letter K, finger 9 on letter L and finger 10 should be placed on semi-colon.

Fig. 1 Positioning of hands while typing

Start Tux Typing

To start Tux Typing, follow the steps given below:

1. Click **Start** menu.
2. Click **All Programs**.
3. Click **Tux Typing (Full Screen)** option from **Tux Typing** menu option. The Welcome screen appears as shown below.

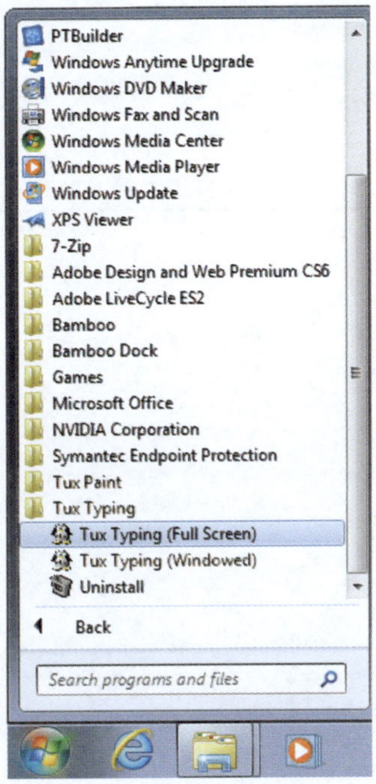

Fig. 2 Tux Typing (Full Screen) option in All Programs

Fig. 3 Tux Typing Welcome Screen

4. The default language of Tux Typing is English. If you want to set any other language, click **Options** from the Main Menu. From the menu that follows, click **Setup Language**.

You will see the names of all languages that are supported by Tux Typing. Click on the desired language.

Fig. 4 Setup Language option

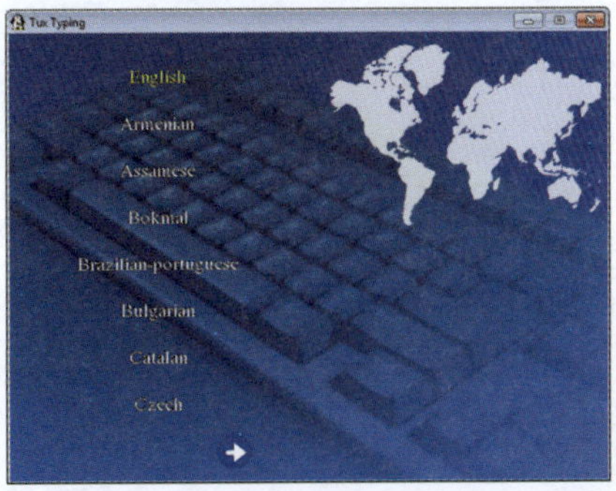

Fig. 5 Various languages supported by Tux Typing

Exploring IT Personalities

Select and write about any two IT Personalities in the space given below. You can also paste their pictures.

1. Tim Berners Lee
2. Sabeer Bhatia
3. N.R. Narayana Murthy
4. Lawrence 'Larry' Page

NOTES

NOTES